FACING CODEPENDENCE

FACING CODEPENDENCE

What It Is, Where It Comes From, How It Sabotages Our Lives

Pia Mellody

with Andrea Wells Miller
and J. Keith Miller

HarperSanFrancisco

A Division of HarperCollins*Publishers*

Library of Congress Cataloging-in-Publication Data

Mellody, Pia.
  Facing Codependence.

  1. Co-dependence (Psychology)   I. Miller, Andrea Wells.   II. Miller, Keith.
III. Title.
RC569.5.C63M45   1989   616.86   88-45662
ISBN 0-06-250589-0

  90   91   92   93   MAL   10

To Jane Kiamy, my surrogate mom,

who first showed me my lack of understanding that I am precious.
She tenderly and repeatedly confronted me about the fact that I am
lovable, cherished me when I couldn't love myself, and shared with
me how her family nurtured her as she developed her own sense
of preciousness.

Contents

Foreword

In certain men and women normal human feelings such as shame, fear, pain, and anger are so magnified that these people are almost always in an emotional state marked by anxiety and feelings of being irrational, dysfunctional, and/or "crazy." Such people also think they should be able to make those around them happy, and when they can't, they feel as if they are somehow "less than" others.

These people often find themselves overreacting to everyday happenings, experiencing feelings far more excessive than appropriate for a given situation. For example, when something frightening happens, instead of normal fear, they experience panic or anxiety attacks. These attacks can also occur for "no reason." When some of life's normal pain comes their way, their experience may be deep despair, hopelessness, or perhaps suicidal thoughts or behavior. And when a situation arises that would ordinarily provoke some genuine appropriate anger, such people sometimes explode into volcanic rage. And during these extreme emotional experiences, they often think, "Why does he treat me this way? Doesn't he know how painful it is to me?" But they cannot control the emotional outbursts and are baffled.

These intense emotional reactions often occur over life's less dramatic experiences, such as a disagreement with one's spouse over which movie to see or where to go on vacation. Despair or rage can be triggered by the disappointment of interviewing for a job and not being hired, the sadness of a good friend's moving to another town, or the anger of the neighbor's dog messing up the flower bed. Any of these experiences can evoke emotional reactions that are far from moderate—they can range from intense explosive feelings to bland sweetness and lack of any emotional expression at all. But both of these seemingly uncontrollable reactions sabotage the lives and relationships of such people.

There is now much documented evidence pointing to the fact that the physical stress of living with pent-up or explosive feelings may contribute to physical disorders such as high blood pressure, heart disease, arthritis, migraine headaches, cancer, and others. This emotional factor of codependence can sabotage our health as well as our relationships.

And yet these men and women operate as if they believe that only by being "perfect" in all they do or by pleasing the people around them can they calm the outsized, uncontrollable, and irrational feelings that tyrannize them. They live in the delusion that the bad feelings (that they sometimes find almost overwhelming) can be quelled if they can just "do it better" or win the approval of certain important people in their lives. By this attitude they unconsciously make those people important and their approval responsible for their own happiness. When those they try to please "don't appreciate what I'm doing for them" and will not give the crucial approval, the emotionally tyrannized individuals become furious. But since the good opinion of the would-be approval giver is so important, this rage must be repressed. And although this rage isn't shown directly, the anger may come out "sideways," in sarcasm, forgetfulness, hostile jokes, or other passive-aggressive behaviors.

Often such men and women appear to be gentle and helpful. A closer examination, however, reveals in them a powerful need to control and manipulate those around them into giving them the approval they believe they need to subdue their overwhelming feelings. But all their efforts are of no use in the long run, because *no one* can take away the overwhelming part of their feelings. They may come to believe there is no hope for them.

On the other hand, in some people with quite similar backgrounds a very different thing happens. The normal human emotions are so minimized that they hardly experience any feelings at all—no fear, no pain, no anger, no shame, and also no joy, no pleasure, no contentment. They shuffle numbly through life from one day to the next.

It was actually the families of alcoholics and other chemically dependent people who brought these two clusters of symptoms to the attention of therapists in treatment centers. These family members all seemed to be plagued with intensified feelings of shame, fear, anger, and pain in their relationships with the alcoholic or addict who was the focal point of their family. But they often were not able to express these feelings in a healthy way because of a compulsion to please and care for the addicted person.

Their efforts were ostensibly to get the chemical dependent sober or free from drugs. However, there were also some common irrational aspects to this relationship between the family and the alcoholic. One irrational aspect was that most of the family members had a deluded hope that if they could only be perfect in their "relating to" and "helping" the alcoholic, he or she would become sober—and they, the family members, would be free of their awful shame, pain, fear, and anger.

But this strategy never worked. Even when the alcoholic got sober, the family often stayed sick and actually appeared to resent the sobriety. Sometimes they sabotaged it. It was as if the family *needed* the addict to stay sick and dependent on them so they could maintain their dependence on him or her in hopes of explaining their exaggerated bad feelings.

In some ways the alcoholic directly or indirectly abused the family members by his or her self-centered behavior. Sometimes the addicted family member would be so physically, sexually, or emotionally abusive that any normal person would have left the relationship. And that's the second irrational aspect in these family members' relationship to the addicted person: they did not leave and seemed to be locked in a joint sickness with the addict.

The family members' continuing to stay in a relationship despite harmful consequence (abuse) paralleled the alcoholic's continuing to drink despite harmful consequences. Thus it became clear that as the alcoholic depended on alcohol to handle the overwhelming feelings of his or her disease, the family depended on the alcoholic in a sick and similarly addictive way. In other words, the alcoholic and codependent were trying to solve identical basic symptoms of the same disease—the addict with alcohol or drugs and the codependent with the addictive relationship.

This codependence with an addict led therapists to the awareness that a painful and crippling disease was in operation—*a disease they later realized was also operating in countless families across America that had no chemically dependent member.*

We believe that these suffering people are in the grip of a serious underlying disease called codependence (or codependency). And only a few of the sufferers know anything about a cure for the crippling symptoms described earlier. Yet people who have codependence often wind up in despair and actually die from its effects. The death certificates never mention the disease by name. Instead the victims' histories tell of hopelessness, suicides, "accidents," cardiovascular problems, and malignant diseases related to self-neglect, stress, and repressed anger and its accompanying depression.

The disease is amazingly difficult to see from the outside because its sufferers wear a mask of adequacy and success designed to win the all-important approval. But these slaves of powerful, seemingly groundless compulsive feelings are doomed to be on an endlesss treadmill of personal failure and intensified experiences of shame, pain, fear, and repressed anger.

In fact many people, in their efforts to flee these overwhelming feelings, turn to chemicals to numb their discomfort. They are set up to become alcoholics or other kinds of addicts. We believe that codependence underlies and fuels these addictions. When an alcoholic or any other addict gets rid of the addictive chemical agent or behavior, then that person will often have to face the consequences and symptoms of codependence on the road to recovery.

During the past eight years Pia Mellody has developed a therapy for codependence at The Meadows, a treatment center for addictions in Wickenburg, Arizona. She has personally led hundreds of people suffering from the agonies of codependence into recovery and wholeness. The purpose of this book is not to give a detailed history of the development of the concept of codependence or arguments concerning its status as a bona fide disease. Its purpose is to describe the disease as Pia Mellody has seen it—from the inside, in hundreds of patients' lives, including her own. (Although all of the authors have contributed to this book, the first-person singular has been used by Pia Mellody to describe the disease and the approach to recovery presented here.)

The therapeutic concepts, methods, and eclectic approach are in the language that has come out of the cauldron of Pia Mellody's experience of fighting the disease and not from a theoretical base. In fact, this is not an attempt to devise or defend a theoretical construct at all. Rather the authors intend (1) to describe the structure of the disease of codependence in terms of the way it operates in everyday life and relationships and (2) to point to a practical model that works in healing people who suffer from the symptoms. For those interested in the history and development of the notion of codependence in the psychological literature, we have provided a brief appendix in the back of this book.

Many of the concepts of this book such as the connection of codependence to child abuse and the description of external and internal boundaries were formulated and first used by Pia Mellody years ago. The fact that some of these ideas have become known and used among therapists and codependents everywhere through her lectures and tape series ("Permission to be Precious") is a tribute to Pia's insights, and we are pleased to be working on this project to present her views of codependence and ours in an organzied written form.

We hope that from reading these pages those who are plagued by this disease will be able to face it and get into recovery*, and because the very acts of facing codependence and moving beyond denial have brought us to the beginning of hope and recovery in our own lives.

Andrea Wells Miller
J. Keith Miller

Breaking Free: A Recovery Workbook for Facing Codependence, by Pia Mellody and Andrea Wells Miller, is also available.

Acknowledgments

I wish to acknowledge the contributions of my husband, Pat, who is an important part of the development of these concepts. The concept of boundaries came from discussions we had about ideas his mother gave him on defending himself. Also, an important reason I have come to an understanding of this material was the result of Pat's confronting my disease process. And as director of The Meadows, Pat made it possible for me to begin working out the ideas by talking with other codependents in treatment and teaching these ideas at The Meadows.

I also wish to thank the hundreds of fellow codependents who shared their stories with me and who tried these ideas as they were developed, reporting their pain and successes back to me. Their cooperation, encouragement, and eventual signs of recovery have served to motivate and inspire me on my own journey.

Recovery from codependence cannot be done alone. During the dark times when I feel cut off from the support of other human beings, I am deeply aware of the supportive presence of a Higher Power, without which I'm sure I would be lost.

Pia Mellody

The authors wish to acknowledge with gratitude the following: Roy Carlisle, who saw the scope of this project and encouraged us to proceed; Thomas Grady, whose direction regarding structure was invaluable; Valerie Bullock, Arlene Carter, Richard D. Grant, Jr., Carolyn Huffman, Charles Huffman, and Kay Sexton whose reading of earlier drafts of the manuscript and comments helped us to clarify these concepts. We also wish to thank David Greene, who helped us with the reference to electrical circuit theory in the discussion of carried shame. Since the final decision regarding wording and editing rests with Pia Mellody and ourselves, they cannot be blamed for any mistakes or confusion still remaining.

Andrea Wells Miller
J. Keith Miller

Introduction: How It All Began

Several years ago, in 1977, I was having an increasing number of problems in my relationships with people who were important to me. My relationship with myself was also painful and difficult; and I was restless and feeling a great deal of anger and fear.

I stayed so busy trying to be a first rate wife, mother, nurse, and friend that I was exhausted. And no one seemed to appreciate the fact that I was killing myself for them. I was a secret people-pleaser and felt a growing sense of rage about that, but I couldn't seem to change or quit worrying. I was filled with fear and felt very inadequate even though I was trying to do everything perfectly. And I was beginning to feel more and more shame because I couldn't seem to actually pull it off and be perfect. Then finally my outer, adequate-looking shell began to crack and blasts of hot anger burst out, frightening me and the people around me. And things got worse. The inner anxiety and pressure I felt were almost "wall to wall."

My life seemed to be going out of control. So I sought help and finally went to a treatment center in 1979 to be treated for a set of symptoms that I now speak of as codependence.

I found that the professional community to whom I had gone for treatment did not know how to help me. It was as if I were speaking English and they were hearing Greek. They didn't appear to understand the nature or seriousness of my symptoms, and the treatment they offered didn't seem to relate to what I was experiencing. I tried to communicate what was happening to me, but I had the sense that I was not being understood or taken very seriously. Instead, I felt that the staff blamed me for what was wrong with me. From my perspective all they did was stare at me as if I were an irrational, uncooperative troublemaker. It was extremely frustrating and I was very angry. I knew I probably *was* irrational, but I also knew that the people at the center did not really understand what was wrong with me.

At that time I worked at The Meadows, a treatment center in Wickenburg, Arizona, for alcoholism, drug abuse, and related problems. Because of my job I had enough knowledge about treatment to know that my therapists did not know how to treat me. I was frightened by that and thought, "If I go to the professionals who are supposed to know what they're doing, tell them what's wrong, and they just stare at me as if they think I'm crazy—I really am lost!"

When I got out of that treatment center and came home to The Meadows where I worked, I was more confused and dysfunctional than before. I had outbreaks of rage at the drop of a hat. I still remember the day a short time later, when the executive director at The Meadows said, "Pia, if you can't stop being so angry in staff meetings, you can't go to the meetings anymore." I knew that meant "you're going to lose your job," which terrified me. At that point I realized my life had become unmanageable and that I had to do something about my condition.

Because of both of these experiences, not being helped in treatment and the possibility of losing my job because I was so angry, I set out on my own journey of discovery. Actually I wasn't that mature. One day I was sort of catapulted into the adventure of discovery by another fit of anger at work. I was in the director's office talking to him and another counselor who was standing at the door. I wanted these two very important men in my life to know how upset I was that nobody seemed to "hear" me when I was telling them about my distress. And as I talked, I realized these two extremely intelligent professionals couldn't understand me either! That memory hurts even today.

They just looked at me and one of them said, "Well, why don't *you* figure out how to treat whatever that is?" I was so furious I wanted to hit them both! I whipped around and stalked out the door while they stared after me as if they thought I were crazy.

As I stormed down the walkway outside the office I remember saying to myself, "If *I* must find a way to treat this condition, all of us who have these problems are sunk. How can I do it?" I felt so inadequate. Even trying to identify what the issues were confused me. As I wrestled with my anger and panic, I wondered how could I sort out the symptoms of my pain and figure out a treatment plan myself.

Then, as I walked around the corner of the building, something happened to me. In that moment it was as if all my confusion were gone and my thoughts focused. A single simple idea filled my mind in the form of a question: "How did the first alcoholics in AA start into recovery?" And the answer came from somewhere inside me, "People shared their experience, strength, and hope. In doing that they learned what their disease was all about, and from that beginning everything else happened."

Then another thought came: "My symptoms may be connected to being abused as a child." I had some profoundly traumatic experiences during my own childhood, and I suddenly remembered that some other people I knew with symptoms similar to mine had been abused as children too. Maybe many of them had been! Maybe all of them had been! I had enough knowledge about psychology and therapy and enough recovery in AA to know that painful childhood experiences were a common snake pit in addictive and other kinds of dysfunctional families. So I told myself that I would interview all the abused people who came into The Meadows for treatment, talk to them specifically about their childhood abuse and their current problems, and see if I could find out how they were affected. We were already doing some basic work in the area of child abuse anyway. I started by asking the counselors if they would send the people who had been abused to my office.

In my work with patients at The Meadows I had come to know that the term "abuse" is much broader than most people think. It includes more than the overt physical beatings, injuries, and sexual incest or molestation we commonly associate with the term. Abuse also takes emotional, intellectual, and spiritual forms. In fact when I talk about abuse, I now include any experience in childhood (birth to age seventeen) that is less than nurturing. In my lectures I often use "dysfunctional" and "less than nurturing" interchangeably with "abuse."

As these victims of child abuse came into my office and shared their experiences, I began to see the connections between their abuse and their intense and seemingly irrational adult symptoms, which were similar to my own. After a while a common picture of what was going on with these different people came into focus. Although I already knew that different kinds of abuse in childhood created different kinds of problems in adults, I could now see clearly that there was a common symptomology in the adult lives of those of us who had experienced abuse as children. We *all* had the symptoms of what we now generally understand to be codependence. (I will describe specific symptoms at length in Part One.)

As I talked with these people about their problems, they (and I) were elated. We understood each other. Somehow we were the *same kind of people* who were talking the same language. What they described sounded clear and not at all like Greek to me.

After we would talk a while they'd say, "What can I do about these crazy feelings, Pia?"

And I'd say, "I don't know but let me think." Then I'd think of something that might help with a certain symptom they were experiencing and say, "Try this and I'll do it too." I don't believe in advising anybody to do anything I am not willing to do myself.

So I started suggesting behavioral experiments for patients to try to help with the irrational feelings and actions that made their lives so dysfunctional and self-defeating. And as I did the things I suggested my patients try, I started feeling better. I realized my own wellness process had begun at last! I had the advantage of sharing with hundreds of people over the next months and years who were in a live-in treatment center for a month to six weeks. They tried what I suggested and gave me immediate and continuing feedback.

The counselors also began telling me that after the patients had spent some time in my office talking on a one-to-one basis about their childhood abuse issues, they seemed to do better in the rest of their treatment. They seemed to settle down and understand more of what was going on with them. So I started writing down the suggestions I was making and noting the effect on the patients.

Later I was to realize that while we codependents are often very sensitive to the problems of the people around us and often have unusual insight into ways to help them, we frequently grope in darkness when it comes to diagnosing and helping ourselves with problems of codependence. So I believe that it was only by suggesting procedures for *other people* and then trying them that I helped myself.

News of the effectiveness of this new approach to isolating and treating the symptoms of codependence started circulating around the community at The Meadows. Before I knew it, more patients were being sent to my office. Since I was the nursing director and not working as a therapist at that time, I was overwhelmed. So I asked the director of the center if I could create a workshop in which I could tell all the child abuse survivors at one time about the relationship between their abuse as children and their adult symptoms of codependence.

That was the beginning of the workshop on child abuse and codependence that I have since conducted both at The Meadows and in different cities around the country. I have been amazed at the positive response to it.*

The concepts in this book and the model for therapy and recovery from codependence I am using have come out of several years of

---

*The workshop is available as a six-cassette lecture entitled "Permission to Be Precious" from Mellody Enterprises, P.O. Box 1739, Wickenburg, AZ 85358.

interviewing patients at The Meadows and the counseling that grew out of the initial interviews. I approach this subject as a messenger with some words of hope rather than as a research scholar who has sifted through all the academic journals. I know personally how it feels to live with the disease of codependence. It nearly destroyed me; I seriously considered committing suicide a number of years ago. But in working with the disease in the lives of hundreds of patients, I have discovered, with the help of these patients, the director, and other counselors at The Meadows, a way to treat the disease that has surprised and encouraged us all.

Most codependents do not understand much about how the disease works in their own lives and how it affects their relationships and their own happiness and self-esteem. Although the disease is rampant in our culture, the state of the art in the healing of codependence is so new and primitive that many therapists don't know how to speak to it. They aren't clear about the cause of the disease or about the best way to treat it. Many therapists and communicators spend much time trying to sort out and define psychological symptoms, which has been of great value, but to date I haven't heard much helpful discussion of the underlying causal problems and how these problems, begun in childhood, stay alive in the symptoms of the adult codependent.

Our purpose is to describe the symptoms in simplified terms. We will show how these symptoms operate in adult lives and relationships, and how they create difficulties and separation in our relationships with ourselves, others, and a Higher Power. We also wish to point out and clarify the less-than-nurturing experiences in childhood that lead to the adult symptoms of codependence.

The sophisticated student of psychology may have some initial reservations about some of the concepts that follow, including the notions of carried or induced feelings and the shame core. I am not entering a debate, but merely presenting a clinically based description of the illness and insights that have already helped hundreds of people begin the journey toward recovery.

This book will cover the following key aspects of the disease as I now see it:

- How codependence operates in the adult codependent: the five primary symptoms involved and the unmanageable consequences stemming from them
- An overview of the disease and its effects, including where it comes from, how it develops, how it sabotages our lives, and how codependents pass it on to their children
- A description of the basic nature of a child and how, depending on whether the child receives functional or dysfunctional parenting, that child matures into a functional adult or codependent one
- A discussion of how the experience of abuse instills in the child the inappropriate (unduly painful, exaggerated, or frozen) feelings leading to abnormal behaviors that create difficult relationships
- A deeper look at various forms of dysfunctional parental behaviors (which I also call "child abuse") that produce codependent adults
- Information about avenues to recovery now available to codependents who wish to do something about this painful life-threatening illness

Facing codependence takes courage. Unlike alcohol and drug abuse victims, codependents have often been *rewarded* for the inordinate amount of people-pleasing they engage in as a result of their disease. But overwhelming fear, anger, pain, shame, and despair have kept many of us miserable in our codependent behaviors for years. And the *only* way I've found to treat codependence effectively is to encourage people to enter courageously the process described in this book. I tell every patient I treat, "The secret to your recovery is to learn to embrace your own history. Look at it, become aware of it, and experience your feelings about the less-than-nurturing events of your past. Because if you don't, the issues from your history will be held in minimization, denial, and delusion and truly be behind you as demons you are not aware of. And this situation will continue to make you miserable through your own dysfunctional behaviors." More directly I tell my patients, "Hug your demons or they will bite you in the ass." In other words, "If you do not embrace what is dysfunctional, you are doomed to repeat it and stay in the pain."

This book is about the courage to face our own reality and about a road to freedom.

—Pia Mellody

FACING
CODEPENDENCE

Part 1

THE SYMPTOMS OF CODEPENDENCE

CHAPTER 1

Facing Codependence

An increasing number of people have recognized themselves in the symptoms described in the following pages. They have begun to desire to change, to clear up the distortions, and to be healed from the painful aftermath of experiencing childhood in a dysfunctional family.

If you are such a person, I want to offer you a great deal of hope. The first major step in changing and clearing up these distortions requires facing the fact that the disease exists in your life. One of the purposes of this book is to describe what the symptoms are, where they come from, and how they sabotage our lives, so that you can learn to recognize codependence operating in your own life.

This disease and its link to various forms of child abuse is a complex subject. Because of dysfunctional childhood experiences a codependent adult lacks the ability to be a mature person capable of living a full and meaningful life. Two key areas of a person's life reflect codependence: the relationship with the self and relationships with others. The relationship with one's self, I believe, is the most important, because when people have a respectful, affirming relationship with themselves, relationships with others automatically become less dysfunctional and more respectful and affirming.

Much has been written about codependence in recent years, and many symptoms and characteristics have been described. My own work tells me that five symptoms form the core of the disease.

Organizing the discussion of codependence around these five symptoms seems to make it easier to grasp how the disease operates. Codependents have difficulty

1. Experiencing appropriate levels of self-esteem
2. Setting functional boundaries
3. Owning and expressing their own reality
4. Taking care of their adult needs and wants
5. Experiencing and expressing their reality *moderately*

WHERE THE DISEASE COMES FROM

I have come to believe that dysfunctional, less-than-nurturing, abusive family systems create children who become codependent adults. Our culture's inherent belief that a certain kind of parenting is "normal" contributes to the difficulty of facing codependence. A closer examination of "normal" parenting techniques reveals that they include certain practices that actually tend to *impair* the growth and development of the child and lead to the development of codependence. In reality, what we tend to call normal parenting very often isn't healthy for the child's development; it is less-than-nurturing or abusive parenting.

For example, many people think the range of normal parenting includes hitting a child with a belt, slapping a child across the face, screaming at a child, calling a child names, having the child sleep with them, or being nude in front of a child who is older than age three or four. Or they think it acceptable to require small children to figure out a way to deal with life's situations and problems themselves, rather than providing a concrete set of rules for social conduct and some basic problem-solving techniques. Some parents also neglect to teach basic hygiene such as bathing, daily grooming, the use of deodorants, dental care, removing dirt, stains, and body odor from clothes, and how to keep them mended, expecting the children to know somehow on their own.

Some parents think that if children are not given rigid rules and swift, severe punishment for breaking them, the children will become juvenile delinquents, teen unwed mothers, or drug addicts. Some parents, after making a mistake such as punishing a child in error because the full facts were not clear at the time of punishment, would *never* apologize to the child for the mistake. Such parents conceive that an apology would be seen as showing "weakness" that might undermine the parent's authority.

Some parents believe, perhaps unconsciously, that children's thoughts and feelings have little validity because the children are immature and need training. These parents respond to a child's thoughts and feelings by saying "You shouldn't feel that way" or "I don't care if you don't want to go to bed—you're going because it's good for you!" and believe they are training the child in a functional way.

Still other parents swing to the opposite extreme and overprotect their children, not making the children face the consequences of their own abusive and dysfunctional behavior. Such parents are often very intimate with their children, using them for confidants and sharing secrets beyond the children's level of development. This, too, is abusive.

Many of us who were raised in homes where this kind of behavior was common grew up in the delusion that what happened to us was "normal" and appropriate. Our caregivers encouraged us to believe that our problems arose because *we* didn't respond appropriately to what happened to us. And many of us arrived in adulthood filled with baffling feelings and with a distorted way of looking at what happened in our family of origin. We got the idea that the way our families behaved toward us was correct and our caregivers were good. This meant by unconscious deduction that since *we* weren't happy or comfortable with some things that went on, we were not "good." Also, we apparently couldn't please our parents by being what we were naturally. This delusion that the abuse was normal and we were "wrong" locks us into the disease of codependence with no way out.

BEGINNING TO TAKE A LOOK

To begin this journey toward recovery each of us must look at the five primary symptoms of codependence and the resulting unmanageable consequences in our lives and begin to reconstruct our individual story about how they came about. The process of facing and identifying these issues seems to be the only way we codependents can begin to change some of the thinking, emotions, and behaviors that have sabotaged our lives.

Most people pass through a period of confusion and painful disappointment in themselves as they recognize the symptoms of codependence in their own lives. This painful part of recovery does not last forever, but we must pass through it to find peace and serenity in more healthy living. We must stop denying the fact of codependence and begin to take responsibility for facing it. After a while, owning and facing codependence becomes less overwhelming and confusing as we move beyond the first stage of recognizing the disease into actively working toward healing from the devastating effects of our childhoods and from living as adult codependents.

The next chapter deals with where I believe each of the five core symptoms of codependence comes from and how each looks in action in an adult codependent's life.

CHAPTER 2

The Five Core Symptoms of Codependence

CORE SYMPTOM 1: DIFFICULTY EXPERIENCING APPROPRIATE LEVELS OF SELF-ESTEEM

Healthy self-esteem is the internal experience of one's own preciousness and value as a person. It comes from inside a person and moves outward into relationships. Healthy people know that they are valuable and precious even when they make a mistake, are confronted by an angry person, are cheated or lied to, or are rejected by a lover, friend, parent, child, or boss. The sense of worth can be felt even when their hair has been cut too short by a barber and even if they are overweight, experience bankruptcy, lose a tennis game, or realize that they have been insulted or gossiped about. Healthy individuals may feel other emotions, such as guilt, fear, anger, and pain in these circumstances, but the sense of self-esteem remains intact.

Codependents experience difficulty with self-esteem at one or both of two extremes. At one extreme self-esteem is low or nonexistent: you think that you are worth less than others. At the opposite extreme is arrogance and grandiosity: you think you are set apart and superior to other people.

WHERE LOW SELF-ESTEEM COMES FROM

Children learn to self-esteem first from their major caregivers. But dysfunctional caregivers give their children, verbally or nonverbally, the message that the children are "less-than" people. These "less-than" messages from the caregivers become part of the children's own opinion of themselves. Upon reaching adulthood, it is almost impossible for those raised with "less-than" messages to be able to generate the feeling from within that they have value.

WHERE ARROGANCE AND GRANDIOSITY COME FROM

Arrogant and grandiose behavior arises out of one of two distinct situations. In the first, a family system teaches its children to find fault with others. The children thus learn to regard others as inferior to themselves. Such children may be criticized and shamed excessively by the caregivers, but they can usually rise above the resulting sense of being "less-than" by judging and criticizing others.

On the other hand, some dysfunctional family systems actually teach their children that they *are* superior to other people, giving them a false sense of power. Such children are treated by the family as if they can do no wrong. They are neither confronted and corrected when they make mistakes nor guided into acknowledging and being responsible for their own imperfection. This kind of treatment is known as "empowering" abuse—these children receive a false sense of superiority over others in terms of value or worth, which sabotages relationships just as much as the message of being less than others does.

OTHER-ESTEEM

If codependents have any kind of esteem, it is not self-esteem but what I call *other-esteem*. Other-esteem is based on external things, including some of the following:

How they look

How much money they make

Who they know

What kind of car they drive

What kind of job they have

How well their children perform

How powerful and important or attractive their spouse is

The degrees they have earned

How well they perform at activities in which others value excellence

Getting satisfaction or enjoyment from these things is fine, but it is not self-esteem. Other-esteem is based either on one's own "human doing" or on the opinions and behavior of other people. The problem is that the source of other-esteem is outside the self and thus vulnerable to changes beyond one's control. One can lose this exterior source of esteem at any time, so other-esteem is fragile and undependable.

I have four children. If any one of them starts to "fail" in some task, project, or relationship at any time, my life can quickly become unmanageable. When I base *my* esteem on their levels of success, I am only experiencing other-esteem. And yet other-esteem is all many of us have.

HOW DIFFICULTY EXPERIENCING APPROPRIATE LEVELS OF SELF-ESTEEM LOOKS IN ACTION

Frank is a very wealthy forty-five-year-old architect who never developed self-esteem, never learned how to value himself from within. He has consequently gathered esteem from the outside and bases most of his other-esteem on the fact that he has a lot of money and influence. When Frank lost his money through an unavoidable slump in the real estate market, he lost his whole sense of esteem and self-worth. Frank came into treatment profoundly depressed, believing that he was now absolutely worthless because he no longer had the money and power he had before. Since he did not have any experience with true self-esteem, he felt inadequate and lost.

James, a wealthy lawyer who was in treatment when Frank arrived, had not lost his money. Though he believed that he was truly self-esteeming, his esteem was actually also based on the amount of money he had. James heard me explain that we experience true self-esteem from inside. I explained that self-esteem originally comes from within because we have been esteemed by our parents for who we are and not what we do. But James still did not understand that the esteem he experienced was other-esteem instead of self-esteem, because the money kept him in a state of delusion about where his esteem was coming from. James was in a much more difficult position than Frank, who could feel his lack of self-esteem and acknowledge it. As long as James had his money, he didn't know that there was a problem or that he experienced low or nonexistent self-esteem. But the *effects* of his denied low self-esteem came out unconsciously in his close relationships.

Having money is one of the most powerful outside-in experiences that masks personal insecurity and lack of self-esteem. James is well defended against making true progress in recovery—and yet his life is miserable because he is addicted to alcohol and to controlling people and has been confronted about it by his boss and family, whom he cannot control. But he cannot see lack of self-esteem as an issue, so he can't face his own codependence.

Liza is a forty-two-year-old mother who esteems herself according to what her children do. When one of her children got in trouble, she lost her sense of esteem. Buddy, her twenty-year-old son, was arrested for selling drugs and wound up in jail. Liza's reaction was an extreme sense of anger; she felt Buddy had taken "respect" away from her. Now she sees herself as the mother of a "jailbird." She presents herself to us at the treatment center as now being "worth less" because her son is having problems.

CORE SYMPTOM 2: DIFFICULTY SETTING FUNCTIONAL BOUNDARIES

Boundary systems are invisible and symbolic "fences" that have three purposes: (1) to keep people from coming into our space and abusing us, (2) to keep us from going into the space of others and abusing them and (3) to give each of us a way to embody our sense of "who we are." Boundary systems have two parts: external and internal.

Our *external* boundary allows us to choose our distance from other people and enables us to give or refuse permission for them to touch us. Our external boundary also keeps our bodies from offending someone else's body. The external boundary is divided into two parts: physical and sexual. The physical part of our external boundary controls how close we let people come to us and whether they can touch us or not. Also, if we have intact external boundaries, we know to ask permission to touch other people and we are careful not to stand too close to them for their comfort. In a similar way, our sexual boundary controls sexual distance and touch.

Our *internal* boundary protects our thinking, feelings, and behavior and keeps them functional. When we are using our internal boundary, we can take responsibility for our thinking, feelings, and behavior and keep them separate from that of others, and stop blaming them for what we think, feel, and do. Our internal boundary also allows us to stop taking responsibility for the thoughts, feelings, and behaviors of others, allowing us to stop manipulating and controlling those around us.

I visualize my external boundary as a bell-shaped jar that fits over me. It's surfaces move out or in as I control distance or touch with others. I visualize my internal boundary as a bullet-proof vest with small doors that open only toward the inside. I am in control of whether they open or are kept shut. And by visualizing these boundaries I can consciously protect myself from the abusive behaviors, statements, or feelings of others.*

A person who has no boundaries cannot be aware of or sensitive to the boundaries of others. Such a person who transgresses others' boundaries and takes advantage of them is termed an *offender*. A *major offender* is a blatant abuser, such as someone who physically beats or sexually attacks others (spouse, children, friends).

With *intact, flexible external and internal boundaries* people can have intimacy in their lives when they choose but are protected against being abused physically, sexually, emotionally, intellectually, or spiritually (unless confronted with a major offender who is more powerful). An intact boundary system is represented by this diagram.

INTACT BOUNDARY SYSTEM

Protection and Vulnerability

Instances of abuse by major offenders are fairly easy to recognize, at least by the victim and onlookers present, but other instances of nonmajor boundary offense may not be so clear.

For example, Marion walks in to a meeting at church and Josie rushes over with her arms outstretched, ready to give Marion a big hug. Marion pulls back, extends her hand indicating she would prefer a handshake, and says, "I'm glad to see you, Josie." But Josie ignores Marion's extended hand and backward step, and grabs Marion in a hug, without asking permission, exclaiming, "Marion, how good to see you!" Josie has just transgressed Marion's external boundary.

---

*A two-cassette lecture by Pia Mellody on boundaries is available from Mellody Enterprises, P.O. Box 1739, Wickenburg, AZ 85358.

In another example, Charlotte comes home from work exhausted and angry about a situation at the office and sees Janice sitting in the living room in her bathrobe watching television. Charlotte says "Good grief, Janice. You make me so angry sitting around in our living room without being dressed. If you wouldn't sit in the living room in your bathrobe I wouldn't be so angry at you!" Charlotte has just demonstrated a lack of internal boundaries by blaming Janice for the anger she is feeling.

Offensive behaviors that demonstrate a lack of external boundaries include insisting on having sex when the partner has already said no and touching others in any way without their permission. Offensive acts that demonstrate the lack of internal boundaries include using sarcasm to hurt and belittle another person, blaming someone else for what we feel, think, or do, or don't do, and believing we are responsible for "making" someone feel, think, or do anything. There are, of course, many other disrespectful and therefore offensive acts that impinge on other people's sense of who they are and what they do or don't do.

BOUNDARIES MUST BE TAUGHT

Very small children have no boundaries, no internal way to protect themselves from abuse or to keep from being abusive toward others. Parents need to protect their children from being abused by others (especially by the parents themselves). The parents also need to respectfully confront the children's own abusive behavior. It is this protection and confrontation by the parents that eventually teaches the children to have healthy and firm but flexible boundaries by the time they reach adulthood.

But people who have grown up in dysfunctional homes usually suffer from various kinds of boundary impairment and are either not protected enough or are too protected. Four basic kinds of impairment result from experiencing less-than-nurturing parenting: (1) no boundaries, (2) damaged boundaries, (3) walls instead of boundaries, and (4) moving back and forth from walls to no boundaries.

NONEXISTENT BOUNDARIES

No Protection

People with *nonexistent boundaries* have no sense of being abused or of being abusive. Such people may have trouble saying no or protecting themselves. They allow others to take advantage of them physically, sexually, emotionally, or intellectually without clear knowledge that they have the right to say, "Stop that. I don't want to be touched," or "I am not responsible for your feelings, thoughts, or behavior."

A codependent with no boundaries not only lacks protection but has no ability to recognize another person's right to have boundaries with the codependent. Therefore, a codependent with nonexistent boundaries moves through other people's boundaries unaware that he or she is doing something inappropriate.

Both the victim and the offender codependent have the same problem, except the victim gets abused while the offender does the abusing. Over the long haul neither can stop the behavior by willpower. Since people with intact or healthy boundaries can't imagine "mature" adults unable to stop abusive or victim behavior, they hold little sympathy for the person trapped in the agony of codependence.

A damaged boundary system has "holes" in it. People with damaged boundaries can at times or with certain individuals say no, set limits, and take care of themselves. At other times or with other people they are powerless to set boundaries. For such men and women there is protection only part of the time. For example, a

DAMAGED BOUNDARY SYSTEM

Partial Protection

person may be able to set boundaries with everyone but authority figures, or his or her spouse, or his or her child. Or the person can usually set boundaries except when he or she is tired, sick, or scared.

In addition, people with damaged boundaries have only partial awareness that others have boundaries. With certain individuals or in certain circumstances they become offenders, stepping into someone else's life and trying to control it or manipulate it. For example a woman may start controlling her niece's wedding after deciding that the bride's mother isn't handling things "properly," whereas this same woman wouldn't dream of trying to control the wedding of her best friend's daughter. Damaged boundaries could cause a person to take responsibility for someone else's feelings, thinking, or behavior, such as when a wife feels shame and guilt because her husband insulted someone at a party. Or perhaps there are certain circumstances, such as being tired, sick, or frightened, in which a person's otherwise healthy boundary fails. For example, a mother may ordinarily relate to her seventeen-year-old daughter with good internal boundaries, allowing her daughter to make her own decisions and live with the results. But after an exhausting week of substitute teaching, baking cookies for the church bazaar, and taking food to the neighbors because of a death in their family, she blames herself for her twenty-four-year-old daughter's decision to break up with her boyfriend and the resulting pain.

WALLS INSTEAD OF BOUNDARIES

Complete Protection but No Intimacy

A system of walls substitutes for an intact boundary and is most often made up of either anger or fear. People who use a wall of anger give off the message (either verbally or nonverbally), "If you come near me or if you say anything about such-and-such, I'll explode! I might hit you or yell at you, so watch out!" Others are afraid to approach for fear of triggering that anger.

People who use a wall of fear retreat from others to keep safe. Such people don't go to parties, don't hang around after a meeting to chat. If this kind of person must be in a group of people, he or she emits an energy field of fear that gives the message "Don't come near me or I'll fall apart. I'm so fragile and afraid that I can't handle contact with anyone." Other codependents in the victim stance understand this and keep away. Unfortunately, an offender is attracted to a person like this as surely as a bull to a waving cape, so a wall of fear is not an effective method of protection from offenders.

Two other types of walls are the wall of silence and the wall of words. The person using a wall of silence becomes quiet and does not emit an energy field of emotion as people using fear or anger do. The person just fades into the woodwork and starts observing what is going on in the room rather than participating. On the other hand the person using a wall of words often just talks right on, even when someone politely tries to contribute to the conversation by making a comment or changing the subject.

It is also quite common for a person to move from one kind of wall to another, switching from anger to fear, words, or silence at any time, though always remaining invulnerable behind the walls.

Moving from Nonexistent Boundaries to Walls and Back Again

Back and Forth from
Complete Protection to None

Moving from a wall to nonexistent boundaries and back again usually happens first when a codependent who uses walls risks coming out from behind the wall and being vulnerable. The person suddenly realizes he or she is too vulnerable and defenseless because he or she has no boundaries. Experiencing life without boundaries is painful whether the person encounters a true offender or someone who is merely taking responsibility for his or her own life (who may seem cold or uncooperative to someone with no boundaries). The exposed codependent experiences this pain and quickly retreats again to whatever wall(s) give protection: anger, fear, silence, or words. The sad thing about walls is that although they give solid protection, they do not allow for intimacy and leave the codependent even more isolated and lonely.

WHERE DYSFUNCTIONAL BOUNDARIES COME FROM

Codependents demonstrate the boundary systems that their parents had. If the parents' boundaries were nonexistent, the children usually do not develop any boundaries either. If the parents had damaged boundaries, the children almost always develop boundary systems damaged in the same way. For example if a woman does not have good boundaries around her husband, it is very likely that her child will not have intact functional boundaries with whomever he or she marries. If one parent had walls and the other had nonexistent boundaries, the child may very well become an adult who shifts back and forth between these two.

HOW DIFFICULTY SETTING FUNCTIONAL BOUNDARIES LOOKS IN ACTION

The description earlier in this chapter of Josie hugging Marion even though Marion indicated she preferred a handshake is an example of Josie's lack of an external physical boundary.

Frank, who has no internal boundaries, is in a turmoil. One week ago, his wife asked him to take her and the children to a local park for a picnic with neighborhood families to celebrate the Fourth of July. Two days later, his mother invited him to bring his family to her house one hundred miles away for a backyard barbecue so she could see her grandchildren. Neither woman knew about the other's invitation to Frank.

With no internal boundaries at all, Frank is unable to take responsibility for what he himself would prefer to do. He is angry and frightened and blames his wife and mother for putting him in this quandary, although the women are unaware of the problem. Frank believes that whatever he decides, he will make one of these two women hurt or angry at him. For an entire week he experiences intense inner pain and can't decide what to do. He finally decides, on the morning of the Fourth of July, to ask his wife to go with him and the children to his mother's house for the backyard barbecue, counting on her understanding and support. But Frank's wife is angry because she planned for the whole week to go on this picnic and she had already bought and prepared all the food. The children are looking forward to seeing their friends and the last-minute change would mean the additional stress of helping the children adjust to their own disappointment. Frank feels guilty, but instead of recognizing and admitting that his indecision and last-minute behavior has created a problem between him and his wife, he blames her for his guilt, believing that if she were more flexible and cooperative, they wouldn't be having this fight. Frank's lack of internal boundaries means he has no ability to see what is really his responsibility and what is someone else's. He often gets mixed up and blames others when he should take responsibility; and he blames himself or irrationally takes responsibility for things that he really has not caused or cannot effect. For example, Frank takes responsibility for the supposed pain and anger he could have "made" his wife or mother feel if he had stated to each of them what he wanted to do.

Don has a damaged sexual boundary. With women other than his wife, Brenda, his sexual conduct is proper. But with Brenda his sexual boundary fails and he often insists on having sex even after she has declined. He continues to hug, snuggle, and give her intimate caresses, ignoring her protests; then he argues and sulks, never realizing that Brenda has the right to say no to sex for that night and that she will quite naturally be angry and hurt that he cannot accept that. If Brenda also has no boundaries, she will probably stuff her anger and go through with the sexual encounter anyway, feeling used and unloved. If she has good boundaries and holds her ground, Don may then respond by punishing her in some way, by pouting, silence, or hostility. Actions such as Don's are not usually termed "offending" or abusive by our culture, but they are acts of a codependent offender who has damaged boundaries with his wife and who thus has little ability to recognize the existence of her boundaries.

Jill has damaged internal boundaries around men she dates. With women and with other men at work, in her family, and friends whom she does not date, Jill has functional internal boundaries and knows what she thinks, feels, and makes her own decisions about what she will and will not do. But when on a date, she "mysteriously" loses that ability and constantly worries if her date will approve of her opinions, her feelings, and her behaviors. She agrees to do things she otherwise wouldn't do just to please a date. For example, she spent a Saturday at a hot, dusty rodeo, cheering enthusiastically at each event, even though she was bored and hated the smell, the heat, and the dirt. And if a date seems to be irritated or depressed, she immediately blames herself, frantically wondering what she could have said or done to bring it on. Because of her damaged boundaries dating is a miserable and baffling experience for this otherwise functional woman.

Maureen is a senior officer at a bank. She is an attractive woman, but on her face is a harsh, glowering look that most people who come near her interpret as seething anger. Her secretary dreads hearing the buzzer that will summon her into Maureen's office, and she limits her comments to her boss, conducting business quickly so she can leave again. When Maureen stalks into the conference room for a meeting, no one greets her or asks her how she is. Others perceive her as very easily irritated and hard to please. Her office is efficiently run and her job is brilliantly done, but she has few friendly associates at the office. She is single and never dates. Her pastimes include watching classic movies on her VCR, going alone to concerts by the local symphony, and taking long solitary walks by the riverbank at her parent's farm outside of town. Maureen uses a wall of anger instead of intact external and internal boundaries to keep people at a physical and emotional distance, to keep her secretary from "wasting time" in her office with "small talk," to keep herself out of political intrigue at work, and to protect herself from being hurt in a romantic relationship. Although she is rarely hurt by people in relationships, she is isolated and lonely.

Kitty, a slim, pale, young woman, is a cook at a fast food restaurant. Kitty is extremely nervous and shy. Occasionally she and a girlfriend, Fran, go to the movies together. Kitty likes Fran, but responds only briefly to Fran's comments, and rarely looks Fran in the eye or voluntarily contributes anything to the conversation. When Fran tells her that she looks nice in her new outfit, she blushes and is tongue-tied. One night after the movie Fran wants to talk and suggests that they stop somewhere for a drink. As Fran talks, Kitty begins to think "Oh no. What am I going to say? What if I can't help her? I never know what to say! I don't understand what Fran sees in our relationship." Kitty stays preoccupied with fearful thoughts about her own performance and can't really listen to Fran, who is sharing her thoughts and feelings. At the end of the evening, because she was afraid and couldn't listen, Kitty still doesn't know any more about who Fran is than she did before Fran talked to her, and Fran feels frustrated and shut out. Kitty has used a wall of fear instead of an internal boundary to keep Fran at a "safe" distance emotionally and intellectually.

People who have built walls of fear may sit at home alone rather than be with people they like. They turn down opportunities to go to parties or even proposals of marriage to people they love, all because they fear that others will get past their wall of defense and abuse them. And the refusals may be expressed in angry or abrupt and alienating terms that are baffling to both parties.

People can use walls of anger, fear, silence, or words in place of external boundaries to control physical and sexual distance and touch with others. And people can use these walls in place of internal boundaries to keep from sharing who they are with other people and to keep from listening when other people share with them.

CORE SYMPTOM 3: DIFFICULTY OWNING OUR OWN REALITY

Codependents often report that they don't know who they are. I believe that complaint is directly related to the difficulty of owning and being able to experience what I call one's "reality." To experience ourselves, we have to be able to be aware of and acknowledge our reality.

Our "reality," as I am using this term, has four components:

The Body: How we look and how our bodies are operating

Thinking: How we give meaning to incoming data

Feelings: Our emotions

Behavior: What we do or don't do

These four parts of our lives constitute our *reality* as I am using the term. When we are experiencing our bodies, our thoughts, our emotions, or our behavior, they make up what is real from our perspective, even if they are not what others would experience in the same situation. So these things are what make each person uniquely who he or she is, and are the "reality" of the person experiencing them.

Codependents have trouble owning all or some parts of these components in the following ways:

The Body: Difficulty "seeing" our appearance accurately or being aware of how our bodies are operating.

Thinking: Difficulty knowing what out thoughts are, and if we know, not being able to share them. Also, giving skewed interpretations to incoming data.

Feelings: Difficulty knowing what we are feeling, or feeling overwhelming emotions

Behavior: Difficulty being aware of what we do or don't do or, if we are aware, difficulty owning our behavior and its impact on others.

Not being able to own our own reality is experienced at two levels: A and B. Level A, the less dysfunctional level, is: *I know what my reality is, but I will not tell.* I hide it from other people for fear of being unacceptable.

Level B, which is more dysfunctional, is: *I do not know what my reality is.* Being level B, is living in delusion (since there is no solid experience of what my reality actually *is*). I must construct or "make up" a personal identity and reality out of what I think I *might be* thinking or feeling, keep silent and not say anything, or try to mirror your feelings and thoughts about me as I can determine them.

WHERE DIFFICULTY OWNING OUR OWN REALITY COMES FROM

Children who live in family systems where they are ignored, attacked, or abandoned for their reality learn that it is not appropriate or safe to express it. They are very likely to have difficulty as adult codependents experiencing and owning their own reality.

Joe remembers an incident when he was four or five years old. Crying, he went to his mother, who was standing at the sink. Even though he held on to her skirt and sobbed into it, she just kept on washing dishes and ignored him. When Joe went crying to his father, his father responded by slapping him—a physical attack. As an adult, it is very difficult for Joe to own or share the fact that he is experiencing pain.

I have a friend who told me that when she and her siblings were simply being needy and expressing it, often by crying, their mother would leave, saying, "I can't stand you. You're causing me to go crazy. I'm going to leave and it is your fault because you cry all the time." My friend learned that expressing her reality resulted in abandonment. There are more subtle emotional versions of abandonment which lead to the same dysfunctional results.

I believe the worst experience for children is to have their reality denied. For example, Fred and Cindy have a terrible screaming argument. Fred calls Cindy a bitch, and she picks up a crystal vase and throws it at him. She misses and the vase shatters against the wall. Their eight-year-old daughter, Molly, who is awakened by the noise, watches from the door of the living room. In the silence that falls after the last shard of glass from the vase clatters to the floor, she says in a tearful voice, "This is horrible and I'm scared. Daddy, you yelled bad words at Mommy, and Mommy, you broke that good vase you told me to be careful about."

Cindy turns to Molly and says, "You're crazy, Molly. Daddy didn't say anything bad to me. There's nothing to be afraid of. And that vase wasn't anything special. If you think that's horrible, then you're wrong. We were just having a normal fight."

Then Fred says, "That's right, Molly. Now you stop spying on us and go back to bed. You shouldn't be up so late anyway."

And Molly thinks, "I think that was horrible and they're telling me it was okay. I must be crazy." In my view, this is severe abuse and can make Molly unsure about her reality in other areas.

As experiences like these are repeated, Molly and Joe lose confidence in their perception and/or stop expressing their reality. They are at level A: they know their reality but won't share it. As the abuse continues and becomes more and more extreme and overwhelming, Molly and Joe detach from their reality, especially their feelings: they quit even feeling the fear and the pain in order to protect themselves from being overwhelmed by their feelings. They have moved to level B, beginning to be out of touch with their own reality, because to stay in touch is unbearable. And they continue to repress those and other painful situations as adult codependents.

People who operate at level B often exhibit the arrogance and grandiosity mentioned earlier. Extreme cases are often called sociopaths in our culture, but some of them aren't. They simply no longer feel the shame associated with low self-esteem. They are what I call "shameless" people who have detached from their own emotional reality (especially feelings of shame) in order to survive the overwhelming abuse of their childhood years. Such people are thus set up to offend and victimize others and it is highly probable that they will do so.

HOW DIFFICULTY OWNING OUR OWN REALITY LOOKS IN ACTION

The Body: Our physical reality is what we look like (attractiveness, body size, grooming standards) and how our body is operating. At level A, I know that when I wear a certain dress I look nice, but I won't admit it. One day when I'm wearing this dress, you may compliment me on how I look. But even though I think that I do look nice, I deny that I have dressed well today, ignore you, change the subject, or point out all the flaws in how I look. At level B I do not have a clear picture of whether I look nice or not in my mind, so when I hear your compliment, I look at myself in the mirror and say, "Why does that person think that?"

Emily, a codependent woman who also has an eating disorder called anorexia, weighs 80 pounds and is 5-feet 10-inches tall. She is on the verge of starvation, but when she looks in the mirror, she sees herself as fat. Emily is at level B and doesn't know what she looks like, *even when she looks in the mirror.*

Some time ago, my husband, Pat, who is director of The Meadows, called my office there and said, "I'm sending a man to your office and I want you to assess him for an eating disorder. He's obese."

I said, "Why do I have to assess him? If he's obese, can't he tell he has an eating disorder?"

And he said, "I can't explain. Just assess it, Pia."

A few minutes later a man walked into my office. He was 5-feet 11-inches tall and weighed 265 pounds. I didn't know that he was the man my husband had sent, so I asked him, "What can I do for you?"

He said, "You need to assess me."

I said, "For what?"

He answered, "An eating disorder."

I then realized what Pat had done. I said, "Are you aware that you're obese?"

"What do you mean I'm obese?"

"How much do you think you ought to weigh?"

"I'm fine at 265 pounds. I'm robust and hardy."

He had no understanding whatsoever that he was obese. He was one of my first experiences with a person who was at level B with his physical reality. He had no concept of how large his body was, just as Emily had no concept of how small hers is. This is a very serious issue.

Some codependents at level B look in the mirror and cannot focus clearly on their own face. They might think they look like someone else or truly not be able to see their faces or bodies.

I personally shift between level A and level B and am at level B concerning what I look like about half the time. When I'm at level B and I look in the mirror, I see my father's face; I don't see mine. When this happens, I don't know what I really look like, and I hate what I see. But when I do know and can see my own face, I like my appearance.

Many of the people I have seen who experience this symptom at level B have been sexually abused. It's often expressd as the experience of being a floating head with no body. Sometimes this is the very first symptom that makes a therapist aware that a person may be an incest or molestation survivor and have the memory of the incident(s) buried somewhere in the unconscious mind.

Thinking: Our thinking process is how we give meaning to incoming data. Data comes into our minds through our senses, so everything we see, hear, smell, taste, and feel through our skin is considered incoming data.

At level A I'm aware of what I think about a given issue, but I won't tell you if you ask me and I certainly won't volunteer it. At level B I don't know what I think, and when you ask me to tell you, my mind goes blank or I get confused and can't tell you.

Jerry and Sylvia are on their way to the movies with Jerry's college roommate, John. John's strong body odor fills the car with a nauseating stench, but Jerry and Sylvia politely converse with John as they drive. When they get into the theater, John goes to the men's room. While he is gone, Jerry asks Sylvia, "So, how do you like my ol' buddy, John?" Sylvia thinks, "I don't like him—he stinks. I wish we didn't have to spend this evening with him, and I'll be glad when it's over." But knowing that John and Jerry are old friends, she can't tell her true thinking for fear of hurting Jerry. Instead she says, "Oh, he's great. I'm glad he could come out with us tonight." Sylvia is at level A with her thinking.

Feelings: Our feeling reality consists of our emotions. At level A I'm aware of what emotions are going on inside my body, but when you ask me what I feel, I don't tell you. I lie and name a different feeling or deny that I'm having any feelings when I know I am. For instance, when I'm really angry about something someone said but don't want to admit that feeling, I might tell the person, "I feel sad that you said that, but I'm not angry."

At level B I am not able to tell you my feelings because I don't experience emotions. Such people will often say, "I'm numb" or "Nothing happens when I try to feel." This is not healthy and is a very serious symptom of codependence.

Behavior: What we've done or not done constitutes our behavioral reality. At level A I remember my behavior clearly, but when asked about it, I report something else or say I don't remember. For example, it's my job to feed the cats at our house. One night, I forgot to do it, and the next morning there they were at the back door, meowing and pacing around. My husband walked in and said, "Pia, did you feed the cats last night?"

Being at level A with my behavior that day, I said, "I can't remember. I think so. Why?" I knew this was actually lying, since I did remember I'd forgotten, but I didn't want my husband to know that. Another way to hide what I'd done would have been to give such a complex and vague answer that he couldn't understand what happened. If I had been at level B, I would have had no conscious awareness of what I had or had not done (e.g., I honestly would not have remembered whether I fed the cats or not).

As another example of level-B behavior, I got a report at The Meadows one morning that Dave, a patient in treatment, called the night nurse, Rebecca, a bitch. Rebecca had turned in the report as she finished her shift. I forwarded the report to Dave's counselor, who confronted Dave in the group that morning. He said, "Hey, I got a report that you called Rebecca a bitch last night. Do you want to talk about that?" And Dave looked amazed and said, "I don't remember that. I don't know what you're talking about." And being at level B, he was sincere.

The fact that patients have been operating at level B regarding their behavior also comes up often during family week, when the families come and tell the patients what their behavior has been. It becomes obvious that such patients are deluded and don't even know they have done certain things. They have repressed them or been in a blackout or just cannot acknowledge that this behavior is part of the problem. These people need the observing family to come break them loose from denial and delusion. Operating at level B is a serious symptom.

CORE SYMPTOM 4: DIFFICULTY ACKNOWLEDGING AND MEETING OUR OWN NEEDS AND WANTS

Each of us has basic needs and individual wants that are our responsibility to satisfy. I identify needs as those things we must have to survive. All people have dependency needs, children as well as adults. The difference between a child's dependency needs and those of an adult is that the child must have his or her needs met initially by his or her major caregiver and be taught how to take care of each one in the course of growing up. An adult is responsible for knowing how to address each need and asking for help when help is truly needed.

The dependency needs I focus on for adults are food, shelter, clothing, medical/dental attention, physical nurturing, emotional nurturing (time, attention and direction from others), sex, and financial resources (earning, saving, spending, budgeting and investing money).

There are some needs that can only be met through interaction with another person, such as physical nurturing or emotional nurturing. But we must be taught that it is our responsibility to recognize those needs and ask someone appropriate to meet them. We in turn must learn to meet others' needs at appropriate times in proper circumstances, which is called interdependence.

I divide *wants* into two categories: little wants and big wants. Little wants are truly preferences. They are things we don't have to have, but when we choose them they bring us great joy. For example, Sherry thought she wanted a terrycloth bathrobe. Whether it would bring her joy or not would determine if she really wanted it. Although she had two other bathrobes, and certainly didn't *need* another one, there was something attractive about terrycloth to Sherry. When she got the new robe, she found that she did get great joy from it. She loved wearing it. Every time she put it on she felt wonderful. The robe was truly a want because it brought her joy.

The big wants take our lives in a general direction and bring us fulfillment. They include such things as "I want to be married to this person." "I want to be a doctor." "I want to develop this corporation." "I want to have a child."

THE FOUR CATEGORIES OF DIFFICULTY ACKNOWLEDGING AND MEETING OUR WANTS AND NEEDS

We experience not being in touch with our needs and wants in one of four different ways according to the experiences we had in childhood.

I am *too dependent*. I know my needs or wants but expect other people to take care of them for me, and I wait, expecting them to know to do so as I do not take care of them myself.

I am *antidependent*. I am able to acknowledge to myself that I have needs and wants, but I try to meet them myself and am unable to accept help or guidance from anyone else. I'd rather go without the thing needed or wanted than be vulnerable and ask for help.

I am *needless and wantless*. Although I have needs or wants, I am not aware of them.

I get my wants and needs confused. I know what I *want* and I get it, but I don't know what I *need*. For example, I try to take care of my needs that I'm unaware of by buying everything I want. Though I may need physical nurturing, I buy some new clothes instead.

Each person may experience needs and wants in a different pattern. For example, I may be unaware of any wants. I just can't think of anything I want. At the same time I may be too dependent with needs, knowing what I need but waiting for someone else to meet those needs.

Not tending to one's needs and wants appropriately is often connected to a feeling of low self-esteem (shame). Whenever the "adult child" feels needy or has a want shame flares at the onset of the experience of needing or wanting. This shame originally came from childhood experiences, when expressing a need or want was met with abuse by a caregiver—even though that memory of abuse has long been "forgotten," is no longer conscious. The adult codependent feels as if he or she is terribly selfish to need or want something, however legitimate it may be.

WHERE DIFFICULTY ACKNOWLEDGING AND MEETING OUR OWN NEEDS AND WANTS COMES FROM

Children who had all their needs and wants taken care of by their parents instead of having the parents teach them to meet their own needs in proper ways usually experience being too dependent in adulthood. The parent became enmeshed with the child by taking total care of him or her and not explaining anything to or expecting anything of the child.

On the other hand children who experienced a parent attacking them for having and expressing needs and wants usually becomes antidependent on reaching adulthood. For example, little Sandi goes to her mom and says, "I need a drink" or "I want a cookie." Her mother says, "Leave me alone, you little brat. You bother me too much. Can't you see I'm watching TV?" And perhaps she slaps her on the leg or physically pushes her away. Sandi learns to be antidependent. She, too, can identify her needs and wants but learns early that to go to someone and ask for help results in being abused. As an adult she no longer asks for help but tries to take care of her needs and wants herself. And often, without anyone teaching her how to do things for herself, her attempts to meet her own needs in adulthood are inadequate and leave her unsatisfied. Since she does not ask anyone for help, the needs that require another person, such as physical nurture and emotional nurture, go unmet. Her posture is, "If I can't do it myself, forget it. I'd rather go without than ask for help."

Children whose needs and wants were ignored or neglected by their caregivers usually experience being needless and wantless on reaching adulthood. Such children were not even aware of their own needs because they never were identified. As adults, they often work hard to take care of the needs of others without giving any attention to their own needs and wants. Occasionally at some level these codependents expect that others will reciprocate and take care of them. And they often get angry when this doesn't happen. But many times the codependents are so needless and wantless that they are not even aware of this expectation. If needs occur to them, guilt often ensues. They are completely deluded about the whole question of what they may need or want and how to meet those needs and wants directly.

Confusing needs with wants is the experience of children who get everything they *want* but almost nothing of what they *need*. Often these are the children of wealthy families in which the parents didn't meet the children's interactive needs (such as physical nurturing and emotional nurturing). But every material thing the children ever wanted and expressed a desire for they got. And so as adult codependents, these people are often unaware of needs. All they experience is wants. And these adults go on to indulge their wants and ignore their needs.

For example, a woman may spend money compulsively on clothes, cars, travel, and beauty treatments, acquiring anything she wants. But she ignores her needs, eats a very unbalanced diet, never exercises or has physical checkups. She may try to meet the need for emotional nurturing (spending time with and getting attention from others) by splurging on a new wardrobe and makeup treatment so that the sales clerks and makeup artist will interact with her.

Adults in this category who come into the treatment center are extremely hard to treat, because they don't have a clue about how to take care of their needs. I used to make inspection rounds of the center property and the patients' rooms. The bedrooms of those who confused needs with wants looked like five-year-olds lived in them, like a cyclone hit them. These people had no idea how to take care of themselves. All they knew was how to get what they wanted through manipulation.

A person who confuses needs with wants may seem like a person who is needless—doesn't know what he or she needs—but is healthy with wants, apparently knowing what the wants are and taking care of them. But such people are often out of control with so-called wants—gambling, sex addiction, compulsive spending, overeating, drinking, or using drugs. They are not meeting wants in a healthy way but are in fact overindulging themselves. These people think, "I want what I want and I don't give a hoot about the cost or what I need." "I need to stop drinking and go take a shower and go to bed, and yet I want this drink—so I'll take it." "I want this drug and I'll use it as long as I want it." "I need to stop eating sugar because I'm diabetic, but I want dessert. Who cares about my needs?" Or they simply may not think about their needs.

HOW DIFFICULTY ACKNOWLEDGING AND MEETING OUR OWN NEEDS AND WANTS LOOKS IN ACTION

I've had to teach myself to notice when I was needy and then make myself take care of my needs. When I first started into recovery, I lived alone and was not in touch with my need for food until I went into a hypoglycemic attack. I was losing weight and moving into anorexia. After about thirty-six hours without eating I'd wind up at the nursing station of The Meadows, where I worked, complaining to the nurse on duty that I was faint and dizzy. One time she asked me, "When did you last eat?"

I said, "Oh, thirty-six hours ago."

She said, "Pia, you need to eat. I'll give you a glass of orange juice, but you know you need to start eating."

My response was, "What? I do?" I could not "hear" her even though I was the nurse in charge and could instantly see the sickness in such behavior in another person. I was needless and wantless regarding food and wasn't conscious of even this most basic need.

Other people who are needless and wantless about food can be hungry but just not take the time to eat. Or they might not know how to eat nourishing, well-balanced meals.

Another need I neglected was clothing. I was unaware that I needed clothes. I hardly had anything in my closet to wear. I have a surrogate mom who has been teaching me how to tune in to my own dependency needs. One day, as she was helping me move into an apartment, she confronted me about not having any clothes. She said, "Pia, where are your clothes?"

I said, "In my closet, Jane."

"No. they're not there."

"I just hung them up five minutes ago. Go in there and look."

She came back and said, "Pia, there aren't any clothes in there."

Finally I walked to the bedroom, opened the closet, and said, "Jane, there are my pair of jeans, my T-shirt, my one good blouse, my pair of slacks, and my five uniforms." (I always had enough nurse's uniforms).

She said, "That's not enough."

"What do you mean that's not enough? That's enough for me." I honestly didn't know what my need was. Eventually I moved up to being too dependent, knowing that I needed clothes but not buying them. Now I buy them, but periodically I still must make myself think about the question of whether it is time to buy some new clothes.

I also have difficulty with my need for physical nurturing. At first, I was needless and wantless with this, too, but became aware of my need with my husband, Pat. I was in the kitchen cooking and he was sitting on the couch doing a crossword puzzle, playing with his parrot, and watching television. As I had every night for months, I went to the door of the living room to start a fight with him.

This particular time he said, "Why don't you come sit on the couch and I'll give you a hug?"

I don't know why I did, but I said, "All right." I sat on the couch, he gave me a hug and I felt better. I went back to the kitchen very confused because I felt better, but I couldn't figure out what had happened.

While I was standing at the stove, it dawned on me that I was fighting with him because I needed a hug and wanted to feel more important than the parrot, television, and crossword puzzle. I wanted Pat to give me physical nurturing to demonstrate my importance. Because I was unaware of that need, I picked fights to eventually get the hug I needed when we made up. This "needless" behavior created a lot of chaos in our relationship.

The last example from my own life is about medical needs. Only a few days after having a carbuncle removed from my foot, I gave an all-day lecture. A bandage protected my foot, but I stood and walked on it for eight hours. By the time I rode to the airport I was limping, but I wasn't aware of the pain. The people who drove me to the airport had noticed my limp and suggested that we get a wheelchair, which I refused by saying, "I don't need that."

At that point I did take a pain pill, but I had gone way past the time the medicine was due to be taken and it was too late. Soon after that the pain became so extreme that I couldn't walk at all. Until the moment when I couldn't walk I didn't know I was in that much pain. I was unaware of my need to care for my foot during my recovery from the surgery and actually *wasn't aware* of a very important need.

CORE SYMPTOM 5: DIFFICULTY EXPERIENCING AND EXPRESSING OUR REALITY MODERATELY

Not knowing how to be moderate is possibly the most visible symptom of codependence to other people. And trying to deal with a person who is always acting at one extreme or another is very difficult for those attempting to relate to a codependent in the same household. In other words codependents simply don't appear to understand what moderation is. They are either totally involved or totally detached, totally happy or absolutely miserable, etc. The codependent believes a moderate response to a situation isn't "enough." Only too much is enough. This symptom has manifestations in all four areas of reality.

The body: Many codependents dress immoderately. At one extreme people dress to hide their bodies, wearing baggy clothes up to the neck and down to the toes, or their clothes are so bland the wearers fade into the woodwork. This seems to be especially true for sexually abused people, both incest and molestation survivors.

At the other extreme, however, are codependents who dress so flamboyantly everybody is staring at them. Or perhaps they dress in skimpy, tight clothing so their bodies are clearly revealed to everyone. I find this also among codependents who have been sexually molested.

Physical extremes may also involve how fat or thin people become or how compulsively neat or sloppy personal grooming habits are.

Thinking: Codependents think in terms of black or white, right or wrong, good or bad; there are few gray areas. They have trouble seeing any options in life; there is only one right answer. In relationships codependents often operate from the belief, "If you don't agree with me completely, you're totally against me."

Solutions for problems are extreme. For example, if George tells Sam about something Sam did that bothered him, Sam's solution to the problem could well be to think he should never see George again in order to avoid offending him.

Feelings: The heart and soul of codependence lies in the difficulty codependents have knowing what their feelings are and how to share them. Codependents seem to have the most difficulty experiencing feelings moderately; they feel little or no emotions or have explosive or agonizing ones.

There are four different kinds of feeling reality that codependents can experience. And until one can recognize these four kinds of feelings and where they come from, life can be very baffling and confusing for a codependent.

1. Adult Feeling Reality

Adult feeling reality is a mature authentic emotional response to your thinking. It is not dysfunctional or codependent. These feelings are usually moderate when you experience them and cause you to feel *centered* within yourself. Your current thinking about your life today creates these feelings. I call this experience acting out of the adult in you.

2. Adult-Induced Feeling Reality

In functional people, adult-induced feelings are the result of a process called *empathy*. As a healthy adult, you can be empathic with someone else as that person shares his or her feelings because you can experience that person's feelings with him or her a little bit. Everyone can absorb feelings from another person. For example, if your friend, sitting in a chair near you, talks about a painful situation in her life and feels it very intensely, you as another adult can feel it too and be empathic. This can also happen if she is in denial about her pain but you can see it in her face or if she is being irresponsible with her pain. But this becomes a problem when you take on too much of your friend's pain and become overwhelmed by her feelings, which often happens to codependents whose internal boundary is either nonexistent or damaged.

So, whenever you are in close physical proximity to another adult who is (a) feeling very intensely, (b) in denial of his or her feelings, or (c) being irresponsible with feelings, you can take on too much of the emotion from the other adult and experience adult-induced feelings. These overwhelming feelings usually cause you to feel *crazy*; the feelings do not make sense to you because they are not your own. Whereas, if you only experience the feeling as empathy at a lower, nonoverwhelming level, you are being functional and empathic.

3. *Frozen Feelings From Childhood*

Experiencing little or no emotion is a position of apparent safety. One way this occurs is that the feelings elicited in a child during abuse are so overwhelming and miserable that the child shuts down or "freezes" the feelings in order to survive.

Another way this might happen is that the child may be attacked physically, verbally, or both for having or showing feelings. Stewart received frequent physical beatings from his father. Whenever his father noticed Stewart crying, he would intensify the beating, saying, "Boys don't cry. Stop that!" So Stewart learned to endure the beatings while cutting himself off from his emotions to avoid a worse beating. The feelings involved are usually anger, pain, or fear.

When a therapist starts helping an adult who experienced this freezing process break through minimization, denial, and delusion, the person often taps into the childhood feelings he or she froze a long time ago. The feelings begin to thaw and often seem to be leaking out through tears—at first only a few trickling from the corner of the eye. This is a very powerful emotional experience. It feels almost overwhelming, and it's different from other adult feelings because when frozen emotions thaw the person feels extremely *vulnerable* and *childlike*. The feelings seem to be very old and the person wants to resist feeling them. The message from childhood accompanies the feelings: "I can't feel this because if I do I will die."

4. *Adult-to-Child Carried Feelings*

Children also absorb feelings such as shame, rage, fear, and pain from the adult who is abusing them. These feelings remain within the person into adulthood and are called "carried" feelings, because they've been carried forward from childhood. The process by which children take on feelings during abuse is explained in chapter 6. When you are having this form of codependent feeling reality, you feel *overwhelmed* and *out of control*.

Because there are four kinds of emotional experiences in an adult codependent, learning to recognize the difference is an important part of recovery. Although you might experience a great deal of pain, it may not be adult pain coming from your thoughts today. It might be adult-induced pain from someone close to you, frozen childhood pain now thawing, or carried feelings from your childhood. Learning to evaluate whether you are experiencing being centered, crazy, vulnerable and childlike, or overwhelmed and out of control will help you sort out which of these four experiences you are having.

Behavior: Extreme behaviors in codependents' lives might include trusting everyone or no one at all, letting anyone touch them or allowing no one to touch them at all. Codependent parents may discipline their children severely or not at all.

WHERE DIFFICULTY EXPERIENCING AND EXPRESSING OUR REALITY MODERATELY COMES FROM

My experience leads me to believe that operating in extremes may come from at least two situations and perhaps more. One is observing and reacting to the behavior of the caregivers who operate in extremes. The other is from the experience of "not being heard" or feeling invisible in the family of origin.

When children see their caregivers being immoderate in matters of dress, in their attitude toward their bodies, in the way they think and solve problems, in the expression of their emotions, and in their behavior, they model their reactions after those of the caregiver. Some codependents who didn't like what mom and dad did do exactly the opposite, but because what they are reacting against is in the extreme, their "solution," the opposite behavior, is also in the extreme.

For example, Clare grew up in a family in which she got beaten for every little thing she did that her parents didn't like. So when she grew up she told herself, "I'm not going to do that." But instead of moderately disciplining her children, she was not willing to discipline them at all, and her children are wild and unmanageable because she doesn't make them follow *any* family rules.

In some dysfunctional families, the children's dependency needs were ignored unless the children behaved in an extreme manner to get attention. Only then would the caregivers respond to the children's needs. As adult codependents these people express themselves in exaggerated ways, thinking that by doing so they will be heard and noticed.

From my husband's perspective, it's as if I think I must explain something to him at a high level of intensity, so he will understand and respond at a moderate level. So he, in reaction to my overselling, discounts everything I say by about thirty percent to compensate for my extremes.

HOW DIFFICULTY EXPERIENCING AND EXPRESSING OUR REALITY
MODERATELY LOOKS IN ACTION

I sensed my own immoderation in expressing my feelings

whenever anyone confronted me. I came to call it having "thin skin," because I'd have one of two emotional reactions. If I was afraid of the confrontation, I'd have an intense experience of no self-worth and I'd cry. If I felt stronger than the person confronting me, I'd go to the other extreme and rage at the individual.

At one time Pat, my husband, was also my boss at work. Whenever I'd go into his office to discuss matters in my department, I'd find him sitting behind his desk, which is fairly big, with his shoulders hunched—braced for our encounter. From prior experience he knew that I would either start hysterically crying or glare at him as if I were going to leap over his desk, take the phone cord, wrap it around his neck, and beat him up with the receiver—all depending on which extreme I happened to be in that day.

I also became aware of my extreme thinking reality as I thought back over solutions I had come up with in my marriage to Pat. Right after we were married, Pat told me it bothered him when I washed his coffee cup before he was finished with his coffee. The first thing I thought (and said) was, "When are we getting divorced?"

He said, "I'm not talking about divorce, I'm just talking about a preference. Would you not clean my coffee cup until I'm through with it?"

As bizarre as it seems, in my extreme style of problem solving, I thought, if the problem is that I am washing the coffee cup too soon, the best solution is to get out of the relationship so it won't happen again.

One night a few years later, I began to experience some recovery regarding my operating in extremes. Pat had told me he thought I was leaving too many lights on in the house. My first reaction was to plunge into an intense sense of no self-worth because he was critical of me and start weeping and feeling sorry for myself. He left and went to the back of the house.

Next I got up to go to the bathroom at the front of the house, and as I walked forward through the house I was careful to turn off all the lights along the way. I thought, "Since I'm not in these rooms we don't need to have the lights on." When I got to the bathroom, the light was off. I didn't want to turn it on because I was afraid I would leave it on and get in trouble. And besides, who needs a light on to do what I had to do anyway?

After a few minutes I heard Pat coming up the hall, stumbling in the dark. I could tell he was angry but I didn't know what it was about this time—until I heard him turning on some lights. Pretty soon he found me in the dark bathroom, and he was obviously angry. He growled, "What are you doing?"

I said, in my typical belligerent codependent way during a fight, "I'm going to the bathroom, what do you think?"

"What are you doing it in the dark for?"

"You don't need a light to go to the bathroom."

"There you go, Pia, you don't have any rheostats. You're either full-blown on or you're completely turned off. Don't you know what moderation is?"

I crept back into the living room and curled up in my wing chair. Then I got this brilliant idea. I figured out a moderate number of lights by counting them all and dividing by three. I decided that for me, if the number of lights on was within that one-third number, that would be moderate. And I wouldn't give a hoot if Pat didn't like my decision. I finally owned my thinking reality as I was learning to be moderate.

Pat came back another night and confronted me about the lights again. I looked at him, didn't plunge into my usual sense of no self-worth, and said, "Well, there are eight lights on, and that's okay with me. If you don't like it, why don't you turn some of them off?"

He just looked at me and smiled. I told him how I had decided about the number of lights, which was a step toward recovery for me.

Some of my decisions after that were, no doubt, also a little strange, but I was learning not to jump into extremes at every point in my day. Because codependents usually have no natural sense of what a moderate change would be, acquiring that sense of moderation may take using somewhat unusual or creative means.

THE WORD "NORMAL" IS MISLEADING

In my opinion using the word "normal" to describe recovery is inaccurate. Normal means "what most people do," and many people do engage in thinking, feeling, and behavior that is not healthy. And often, what is considered normal parenting in our culture is actually much less than nurturing to our children. So instead of "normal behavior versus abnormal behavior," I use "functional behavior versus dysfunctional behavior." Functional behavior is healthy.

People who swing to a polar opposite of a dysfunctional behavior to find recovery are invariably disappointed. This is because *the opposite of dysfunctional behavior is more dysfunctional behavior*, and that's not recovery. Functional behavior is somewhere near the center between two extremes.

When you begin to experience recovery and start acting moderately, for a very long time it will *feel like* you're not doing it right. In fact, instead of using the word "functional" when I'm working on this particular aspect of recovery, I use the word "moderate." We know that if an alcoholic is not drinking, he or she is in at least some form of recovery. In a similar way when a codependent is expressing reality moderately, he or she is evidencing some measure of recovery.

CHAPTER 3

How the Symptoms Sabotage
Our Lives

During my recovery process I realized that the five core symptoms described in the previous chapter were sabotaging my relationships with others and with myself. The types of sabotage I identified are:

- Negative control: we give ourselves permission to determine someone else's reality for our own comfort.
- Resentment: we have a need to get even or punish someone for perceived blows to our self-esteem that cause us shame about ourselves.
- Distorted or nonexistent spirituality: we have difficulty experiencing connection to a Power greater than ourselves.
- Avoiding reality: we use addictions, physical illness, or mental illness to avoid facing what is going on with us and other important people in our lives.
- Impaired ability to sustain intimacy: we have difficulty sharing who we are with others and hearing others as they share who they are with us without interfering with their sharing process or with what they share.

I will speak of these areas of sabotage as "secondary symptoms" of codependence, since each results from one or more of the primary or core symptoms of the disease. While the primary symptoms affect codependents *internally*, the secondary symptoms affect their *relationships with others*.

NEGATIVE CONTROL

I am convinced that our frustration and confusion as codependents stem primarily from our attempts to control the reality of other people and from letting their reality control us. Remember that a person's reality is made up of the body, thinking, feelings, and behavior. "Positive control" takes place when I determine my own reality apart from the reality of others. With positive control, I establish for myself what I look like, think, feel, and do and not do. As a healthy person I am "in control" of my reality, of knowing what it is, embracing it, and expressing it when it's in my best interest to do so. Positive control is recovery—the opposite of negative control.

Negative control of reality happens whenever I give myself permission to determine for another person what he or she should look like (including dress and body size), or think, feel, and do or not do.

On the other hand *allowing someone else to control me* is also part of the problem of negative control. Whenever I fail to determine for myself what I look like, what I think, what I feel, and what I do or don't do, and allow someone else to control any of those things for me, I am participating in negative control.

For example, Jack's neighbor was ill and couldn't do any physical work at all, so Jack went over to help out. Jack began by shoveling some bark mulch into a wheelbarrow so he could take it over to spread beneath a tree. The neighbor walked over and said, "Jack, you'd better slow down. You're going to wear yourself out shoveling that fast and then you won't be able to finish the job." At that moment the neighbor was trying to exert negative control of Jack's behavior, telling him how fast he should shovel.

Jack smiled and said, "Don't worry, I've set a good pace for myself. It's a form of aerobic exercise and I'm enjoying it. I'm sure I'll be able to finish this job." Jack used his internal boundary to respond with positive control, determining his own thinking, his own emotional response, and his own behavior concerning the speed of shoveling. He was able to avoid being controlled while politely and cheerfully communicating his reality to the neighbor.

If Jack had not had internal boundaries, he could not have owned his thinking and shared it with his neighbor so calmly. He might have either used a wall of anger and snapped something at his neighbor, or slowed down and allowed his neighbor to control him, feeling anger but not expressing it. In either case, Jack would have been participating in negative control by allowing his neighbor to decide how he would behave.

NEGATIVE CONTROL AND THE CORE SYMPTOMS

Inappropriate levels of self-esteem: Whenever I'm having problems esteeming myself and you have an opinion about me that I don't want you to have, I try to control what you think about me so that I can feel good about myself (or esteem myself). I may do this by arguing, rationalizing, or denying evidence for your opinion.

Impaired boundaries: Whenever I don't have good boundaries, I can't tell where my reality stops and someone else's reality begins. My reality blends with the other person's and I think I can tell that person how to think, feel, and behave because he or she is an extension of me. This can be very irritating to the other party. On the other hand I may think I can read the other person's thoughts and feelings and choose my behavior based on *my perception of the other person's opinion of me*, thereby being controlled by that person.

I am most likely to give myself permission to control your reality in the areas in which my boundaries do not exist. If my *external* boundary is nonexistent or damaged, I give myself the right to tamper with you physically or sexually. For example, I touch you the way I want to touch you or keep my distance the way I want to without considering your comfort level but thinking only of mine. At the other extreme, I will not take care of myself by telling you how close you can stand to me and whether you can touch me or not. Negative control is happening when I either determine what I can do with you physically without your permission or give you permission to tell me what you can do with me physically when it's not in my best interest to let you do that.

If I have a damaged or nonexistent *internal* boundary, there are also two extremes: I either give myself permission to tell you what to think, feel, do, or not do, or I believe I must let you tell me what I should think, feel, or do.

Difficulty owning reality: When I don't know who I am I may expect my husband to determine who I am for me without his being aware that I'm doing this. At the same time I must control who he thinks I am so I can fulfill his expectation and still be who I think I want to be. It sounds crazy, but many of us try to convince someone that we are a certain kind of person so we can believe that we are.

Difficulty meeting needs and wants: If I have trouble taking care of my needs and wants, I will attempt to control your behavior to compel you to read my mind and take care of the need or want for me, so that my needs and wants get met. And I'm usually angry or blaming if you don't "think enough of me" to read my thoughts and take care of these needs.

There are three exceptions to this general definition of negative control. First, parents must influence their child's reality. When a child exhibits dysfunctional ways of dressing, thinking, feelings, or behavior, the parent must help the child express himself or herself more functionally. This may look like negative control on the surface, but when it's done respectfully, moderately, and with good reason, it's part of a functional parent's role.

Second, when people hire a therapist, they are buying the therapist's ability to influence their reality. The therapist's job is to tell the client when, in the therapist's opinion, the client's bodily appearance, thinking, feelings, or behavior is skewed in some way. The therapist's job at that point is to influence the client's reality. It could appear to be negative control, but because it is clearly the purpose of therapy, it is excluded from the category of unhealthy negative control (unless, of course, the therapist is practicing some sort of abusive or offending behavior).

And third, when you have asked someone for an opinion about your reality (such as a sponsor or a friend), the person has permission to tell you. This does not represent negative control, because the person has your permission to influence your reality by his or her opinion.

RESENTMENT

Resentment is holding on to anger at someone, clinging to a need to have the person hurt or punished to make up for the suffering I think he or she has caused me. The person I resent becomes my Higher Power as I think obsessively about what he or she did to me and how I can get even, all the time recreating the shame-filled or pain-filled episode in my mind.

But as I set out to accomplish my goal of getting revenge or punishing, I get the opposite of what I want. The intensity of my anger and my need for revenge or punishment drives away from me not only the person who triggered my shame, pain and anger, but also those I want close to me. This creates an even greater sense of isolation resulting in increasing shame, pain, and anger. In my opinion the need to get revenge or punish comes from the belief that if I can sufficiently punish the person, I can keep this painful experience from ever happening to me again. This immature thinking developed in my childhood when I was unable to protect myself. But as an adult, I do have the ability to take care of myself. I must shift away from the immature thinking and fanticizing revenge into more rational thinking about what has happened.

I believe that everyone is conducting their lives out of what they perceive to be the right thing to do for themselves. Our injuries from others often result from their need to take care of themselves, rather than their desire to hurt us. Such people are usually not aware that they may be taking care of themselves offensively and inappropriately. But we, in our immature way of thinking, believe *they are aware* and that they have deliberately set out to hurt us. As we mature, we gradually begin to accept this concept that we are not always the cause and center of other people's behavior and thinking. Instead of defending ourselves by getting revenge or giving punishment to such people, we understand that much of the time they are actually attempting to take care of themselves. By using our sense of our own reality (thinking, feeling, behavior) and boundaries, we also take care of ourselves by acting in our own best interests when we are around these people. For example, if they have acted abusively or transgressed our boundaries—for whatever reason—we can stop giving information to them, or keep them out of our lives and not spend that much time around them.

Forgiving a person who has hurt me means that I give up the need for revenge or punishment so that I can feel good inside myself. It doesn't mean that I must keep the person in my life constantly battling to protect myself and being hurt in the process. It doesn't mean I approve of the person's actions. It just means I simply acknowledge my feelings, stop replaying the event in my mind, and give up the idea of revenge or punishment.

RESENTMENT AND THE CORE SYMPTOMS:

Inappropriate levels of self-esteem: If I perceive that a person has offended me (whether the offense is real or imagined), I experience a blow to my self-esteem that causes me shame about myself. This is because I believe that I am being treated as if I have no worth. I then have a great need to punish the person so that my value can be restored. Since I have difficulty feeling worth from within I resort to "paying people back" or devaluing them to restore the self-esteem I perceive has been taken from me.

If I am operating from the better-than position and someone

offends me in some way, I believe it is my right to be angry and offend back so I can right the wrong.

Impaired boundaries: With no boundaries, I may often be offended because I am powerless to stop it. Whenever I believe that my boundaries have been transgressed, I experience anger, fear, and pain. At these times resentment may enter in—a need to get even. I am exposed to opportunities for resentment to occur in me more often than I would be if I had functional boundaries and could protect myself from being offended.

Of course, even when I have healthy boundaries an offender more powerful than me may transgress them anyway. I may feel pain, fear, and anger. But resentment—the desire to punish or get even—is not the same as feeling pain, anger, or fear, and I can avoid resentment if I am in recovery.

Difficulty owning reality: There are at least three possible ways that this symptom can contribute to our experiencing resentment. First, as a codependent, I often experience inaccurate or skewed thinking; I am very likely to misinterpret something that happens between me and another person and think I have been wronged or insulted even though I have not been. The skewed thinking creates more opportunities for experiencing resentment. I am as likely to experience resentment on these occasions as I am if someone has really wronged or insulted me.

Second, when I have difficulty figuring out what I think or feel, or difficulty revealing what I think or feel even if I know what it is, I cannot fully acknowledge the impact of a person's behavior on me. I may feel pain, fear, or anger about my perception that I have been wronged or insulted, but not be able to recognize it or express it in a healthy way. My unconscious or unacknowledged thought may be that the person "deserves" to be punished or I "deserve" to get even. If I am not aware that I am thinking in terms of resentment (because I cannot figure out what I am thinking), the result may be baffling, irrational, hostile thoughts, feelings, and behavior toward the perceived offender.

And third, when I can't own my own thinking about myself, I use the opinion I think others have of me to define myself to me. When another person doesn't think what I want him or her to think about me, I may experience resentment. For example, I may get a new haircut. Since I can't own my own thinking, (that the haircut is wonderful), I can't enjoy it unless my husband likes it. But he may tell me that he doesn't like my new haircut, undermining my own concept of myself that depends on his opinion. I may lie in wait for opportunities to get even by belittling or criticizing him in return because he "spoiled" my enjoyment of my new haircut by telling me he doesn't like it. And I have let my difficulty owning my own reality sabotage my enjoyment of my new "look" and my relationship with my husband.

DISTORTED OR NONEXISTENT SPIRITUALITY

Spirituality is the experience of being in a relationship with a power external to and greater than self that provides acceptance, guidance, solace, and serenity. Human beings were not created as perfect creatures, yet many of us get the message that we're supposed to be and that we are defective or inferior when we're imperfect. But when we can acknowledge and embrace the concept that we are imperfect, and that's the way we're supposed to be, then we are what I call "perfectly imperfect."

I believe the experience of being "perfectly imperfect" is felt as joy-filled pain or pain-filled joy that comes about as a result of sharing our imperfection with others and being there for another to share his or her imperfections with us. At the time of the joy-pain there is a sense of being connected to the other person and to a power greater than self that transcends understanding.*

There are two specific ways our lives are sabotaged with regard to spirituality: I have (1) difficulty experiencing a power greater than

---

*A four-cassette lecture by Pia Mellody on spirituality is available from Mellody Enterprises, P.O. Box 1739, Wickenburg, AZ 85358.

myself and (2) difficulty sharing with others who I am or hearing who they are. They are intermingled in the following way.

When I can own my imperfections, share them with another human being, and accept myself as I am—a perfectly imperfect person—I can be open to feeling connected to my Higher Power. Although I'm aware of my imperfection and problems, I can go to my Higher Power for help and guidance.

Sharing my imperfection with myself means that I can admit to myself that I have worth (even though I am imperfect) and have joy about my worth but also experience pain when I know that my imperfection causes trouble for me and for others in relationship with me.

When I can't embrace myself as a "perfectly imperfect" person but buy the notion that I am defective or inferior when I'm imperfect, I'm not open to spirituality. Either I believe that I am perfect (or deny that I am imperfect), which makes me act as my own Higher Power. Or I may believe that I am abnormally imperfect, which results in my not being able to tolerate sharing my imperfections with anyone else because they are so awful I know I'll be abandoned by whomever I share them with—including sometimes my Higher Power.

DISTORTED OR NONEXISTENT SPIRITUALITY AND THE CORE SYMPTOMS:

Inappropriate levels of self-esteem: If we believe we are worthless and "less-than," we may feel that we are not worthy to relate to others or a Higher Power; also, we can't stand the extreme level of shame that comes when we recognize and try to share our own imperfection, and this extreme sense of shame makes us feel alienated from others and a Higher Power. On the other hand, if we are arrogant and grandiose, we become our own Higher Power and do not need an external Higher Power. Either way we sabotage our hope for spiritual recovery.

Difficulty owning reality: To have a spiritual experience, we must be able to share our imperfection and fallibility and listen to others share theirs. If we have not learned to own our reality, it follows that a nurturing spiritual relationship with a Higher Power who would help us deal with our imperfections is almost impossible, because we have a distorted view of our imperfections or we can't get in touch with them at all.

AVOIDING REALITY

As a result of experiencing abuse in childhood we spend a lot of energy in adult life trying to avoid encountering the intolerable reality from the past. But the unpleasant reality is within us anyway. At one level we know and feel something about it and we've known and felt something about it before — even if we can't consciously face and describe it. And the presence of this repressed reality makes us tend to avoid unpleasant feelings in the present.

As codependents, we are immature people in adult-looking bodies. Our physical bodies look adult, but our inner feelings and thinking are immature, fearful, and confused. The difference between our external appearance and internal reality generates stress and pain difficult to deal with. Codependents often drift into an addiction, physical illness, or mental illness to medicate or remove these painful feelings.

ADDICTIONS

I believe that for some people, addictions are an outgrowth of core symptoms of codependence. Any process that relieves intolerable reality can become an addictive process. Substances or behaviors that relieve our distress become a priority in our lives, taking increased time and attention away from other important parts of our lives. And eventually the relieving substance or behavior can lead to harmful consequences that we often choose to ignore since we don't want to give up our pain reliever. We can learn to medicate our unwanted reality through one or more addictive processes, but these processes become destructive forces with lives of their own.

Alcoholism, dependency on other chemicals, overeating, and other addictions are diseases unto themselves, but there are also codependence-induced drinking, drug using, overeating, and so on. I believe codependents sometimes initially use alcohol, drugs, food, and other compulsions to medicate this extra painful reality that most noncodependents do not experience. And later on the codependents may become addicted to the substance they're using as a result of medicating the pain and shame that comes from their codependent problems.

I strongly suggest that men and women in recovery from chemical dependency take a look at whether or not they are codependent as well as addicted. If addicted people are codependents and not aware of the traits of codependence in their lives and the need to recover from them, it is difficult for them to work the steps necessary for recovery from their addiction(s). If alcoholics or addicts do succeed in staying free from substance abuse, they may be very hard to live with and probably quite miserable themselves unless they get in recovery from codependence as well as the chemical addiction. It is vital to the recovery process, however, to first get sober, clean, or abstinent, so that whatever feelings have been medicated can come forth and be owned and looked at.

PHYSICAL ILLNESS

If for some reason we don't indulge in an addiction for relief, our unacknowledged and unmedicated feelings will very likely express themselves in some less conscious and less traceable form. The *Diagnostic and Statistical Manual of Mental Disorders* (*DSM*) refers to these physical expressions of stress as somatoform disorders. These are persistent chronic symptoms for which the doctors can find no cure. Many people come up with one physical illness of this type after another. I believe it is the stress of avoiding the pain of owning our own reality and not learning to appropriately experience and express our feelings that produce many of these symptoms.

MENTAL ILLNESS

The reality of what happened in childhood can be extremely traumatizing and horrible. To survive, some people have to keep themselves from fully knowing about and experiencing feelings about that reality. At some level these people are so afraid this very painful reality will come up into their conscious life that they unconsciously "restructure" their mental world in very skewed ways to avoid the pain of dealing with what is or was. And this "restructuring" manifests itself as mental illness or psychotic behavior. The idea of this restructuring process is that if I can live outside the realm of normally accepted reality, the horrible things I can't face that happened to me in the past simply don't exist for me any longer, and if they did happen they no longer matter.

AVOIDING REALITY AND THE CORE SYMPTOMS

Inappropriate levels of self-esteem: An addictive process can be used to medicate the pain of feeling less than other people. On the other hand the arrogant, grandiose abuser may become addicted to avoid the pain of loneliness and shame that threatens to surface and blow his or her image of superiority.

Difficulty owning my reality: To avoid knowing or feeling emotions about what was or what is, I medicate the feelings, my body expresses them through physical illness, or I become mentally removed from certain aspects of reality.

IMPAIRED ABILITY TO SUSTAIN INTIMATE RELATIONSHIPS

One of the hallmarks of codependents is that we have difficulty in relationships with others (and with ourselves and a Higher Power). Intimacy means that I can share myself with you and let you share yourself with me without either of us trying to change who I am or who you are. Intimacy also involves an exchange. One person is giving and the other is receiving. Sometimes both occur at once. When I say to you, "Can I give you a hug?" I am approaching you and nurturing you. When I say, "Would you give me a hug?" I am asking you to approach me and be intimate with me. During a hug both of us are being physically intimate, but one of us is giving and one is receiving, depending on who asked for what.

Intimacy with another can be experienced in each area of reality: We can exchange touches, both sexual and affectionate on a physical level. We can share our thoughts and feelings. And we can share behavior, by acknowledging to one another what we've done and not done.

AN IMPAIRED ABILITY TO SUSTAIN INTIMACY AND THE CORE SYMPTOMS

Inappropriate levels of self-esteem: If I am in the "less-than" position, I believe you are more important than I am. When I compare myself to you, I come up short, so I cannot honestly share in a way that would be intimate because I fear you will find out how inadequate I am. If I am in the "better-than" position, I often send out messages that I am judging and condemning you, making it unsafe for you to be who you are and thus unsafe to risk being intimate with me.

Impaired boundaries: When I am being either victimized or offensive in a relationship, intimacy is blocked. I also cannot hear who you are, hear what you think I am, or share who I am without an internal boundary.

Difficulty owning reality: I cannot share myself with you if I cannot acknowledge what I think, feel, or do. And if I need you to define my self for me, I try to change what you think, feel or do in order to have the definition of myself that I want. And obviously this dishonest and manipulative behavior does not allow true intimacy to develop.

Difficulty meeting needs and wants: If I am too dependent and rely on you to meet my needs and wants, intimacy bogs down because you become my caregiver and I become dependent and childlike. Our relationship then becomes a parent-child relationship and we can't relate on an adult level.

If I am antidependent and never ask for help, intimacy is blocked, because I cannot share with you what I need or want. If I am needless and wantless, I am not taking care of myself. I then get out of touch with who I am and have less and less of my reality to share.

Difficulty experiencing and expressing reality moderately: If I blast you with my intense emotions, expose you to my extreme solutions to problems, or threaten you with my bizarre behaviors, intimacy cannot flourish. Even though I am sharing who I am, it is so intense and frightening and has the effect on you that I am trying to change you—a behavior incompatible with true intimacy. And the stress of relating to me when I am like this is overwhelming to you, making intimacy highly unlikely. If I, on the other hand, bore you or shut you out with my lack of emotions, intimacy dies. If I am thinking, feeling, and acting at an immature level, a romantic relationship can be turned into a pseudo child-parent relationship, making adult intimacy impossible. If I act, think and feel at an overly mature, controlling level, the romantic relationship also can be turned into a pseudo adult-child relationship. True adult-to-adult intimacy relies on spontaneity, fun, responsibility, respect, and many other things that are difficult when I am living life in extremes.

WHERE DO THESE SABOTAGING SYMPTOMS COME FROM IN OUR HISTORIES?

To get in recovery from codependence it is necessary to look at the source of these symptoms so that we can begin to understand their power in our lives. Many codependents think that their over-reaction or frozen feelings are just "the way they are," and they look for techniques or social skills to help them overcome these personality quirks. But I believe that looking at our histories, identifying the specific incidents about which we had our original overwhelming feelings, and finding a way to own and release those feelings can bring freedom from the sabotaging cycle that makes our lives so unmanageable and painful.

Part two explores the nature of a child and describes how both functional and dysfunctional families affect the maturation process of children. In the following pages you can begin to survey your own childhood experiences, looking for the incidents that led you to develop into a codependent rather than into a mature adult.

Part 2

THE NATURE OF A CHILD

CHAPTER 4

A Precious Child
in a Functional Family

When children are born, they have five natural characteristics that make them authentic human beings: children are *valuable, vulnerable, imperfect, dependent,* and *immature.* All children are born with these attributes. Functional parents help their children to develop each separate characteristic properly, so that they arrive in adulthood as mature, functional adults who feel good about themselves.

CHART I: Development of a Child's Natural Characteristics into Mature Adult Characteristics

Natural Characteristics of a Child	Mature Adult Characteristics
Valuable	Self-esteeming from within
Vulnerable	Vulnerable, with protection (functional boundaries)
Imperfect	Accountable for imperfections and spiritual. Able to look to a Higher Power for help with imperfections
Dependent, (needing, wanting)	Interdependent and able to get needs and wants met appropriately
Immature	Mature at own age level

In addition, children have three other qualities that make it possible for them to mature properly or to survive and cope in spite of remarkable abuse: (1) children must be centered on themselves to develop internally; (2) they are full of boundless energy in order to do the very hard work of growing up; and (3) they are adaptable, so that they can easily go through the maturation process that requires constant adjusting and change. A functional family accepts these traits in their children and supports the children as they move through each stage of development.

A CHILD IS VALUABLE

A functional family values no family member or outside person more than it values its children, and children are valuable merely for being born. They don't have to *do* anything to have worth in the family. However, the family does not value any one child in the family *more* than any other member either. All the members of the family are equally valuable.

At the beginning of their lives, children have no self-concept at all and are like blank slates on which the lessons of "how to live" will be written. They don't yet have any patterns of behavior in terms of personality development. They learn usually by interacting first with Mom and then with Mom and Dad. Children absorb the esteem parents have for them, and this internalized esteem from parents becomes the basis of self-esteem. Healthy children can esteem themselves as their parents esteem them—based on their very existence, not by their "human doing." They know, "I was born precious. I am enough. I am adequate."

HOW A FUNCTIONAL FAMILY SUPPORTS CHILDREN'S VALUE

Bobby was born into a functional family system. His parents treat him as precious and by the time he is an adult he will have learned to generate for himself his own preciousness, his own inherent sense of value. This will have come through functional parental training.

For example, one night Bobby's mother says in a calm but firm voice, "It is now 8:30 and time for you to go to bed."

Bobby says, "I don't want to go to bed."

And his mother replies, "I understand that you don't want to go to bed. But you need to go to bed because you're only eight years old and you need a lot of sleep. You've got a big day tomorrow. I know that this is the right thing for you do to, even though I understand you don't want to do it. It's okay not to want to do it. But here are some different ways you can choose to get to bed and you may use the one you want" (i.e., you can go on your own or I'll help you).

I call this sharing power with the child. The parent *avoids* the dysfunctional stance of saying no to the child and yes to himself or herself, which says to the child that "you can do only what I want you to do and not what you want to do." It gives the child some freedom of choice within a nurturing structure (it is nurturing to get enough sleep by going to bed), which is a power-sharing approach to conflict between the parent and child.

In this functional family, the mother's response is respectful in several ways:

- She acknowledges that she heard what he said about what he wanted and how he felt.
- She gives him the rule and the reason for it.
- She tells him how she will help him carry out the rule by giving him options about how he will go to bed.
- She carries out what she has told Bobby she will do, and when she does, she is physically firm with him, but not hurtful. She either picks him up and carries him or takes him by the arm and escorts him into the bedroom, where she insists that he get into the bed.
- If Bobby did not respond in some positive way to the news that it was his bedtime, then he might have some unpleasant consequences the following day based on the fact that he

stayed up too late and didn't get enough sleep. The consequences fit the nature of what he did or did not do regarding
the family rule. For example, he may have the consequence
that he might not get to do something after school because he
didn't get enough rest the night before.

Because the rule is human, makes sense, and there's a reason for it,
the parent still parents or, in other words, insists that the child take
care of himself. As Bobby's mother parents him in this respectful,
yet structured manner, as if he has value, Bobby begins to esteem
himself from within, begins to develop self-esteem.

In addition, Bobby learns that life's problems present choices.
Many codependents have lost the concept of choices and think they
have "no choice" in certain matters. And the child is introduced to
the concept that power can be shared with someone else. Later on
in life, if Bobby is married and he and his wife cannot agree, they
can negotiate options about how they can share the power or "com-
promise" regarding a specific issue.

A CHILD IS VULNERABLE

Children do not have fully developed boundary systems and
have to rely on their parents to protect them. They are extremely
vulnerable and need the protection of caregivers in the physical,
sexual, emotional, intellectual, and spiritual realms. They learn
how to protect themselves and choose safe times to be vulnerable
in relationships by experiencing the protection and the vulnerability
of functional caregivers. By protection I mean both that the
caregivers recognize and respect children's rights to their own bodies, thoughts, feelings, and behavior even while they guide them
into more functional reality and that when someone else (e.g., a
neighbor, teacher, or older child) behaves in an abusive way toward
their child, the caregivers step in and give protection. They do not
side with the offender against the child.

And the child will also see the parents being vulnerable and sharing and will learn appropriate times in which to be intimate with functional boundaries.

HOW A FUNCTIONAL FAMILY PROTECTS A CHILD'S VULNERABILITY

Susan's parents are functional adults who have boundary systems that permit them to be appropriate with her. Boundaries protect all parts of Susan's reality. Her caregivers don't attack Susan and are appropriate with her physically, sexually, intellectually, emotionally, and behaviorally. Each of her parents take great pains to demonstrate a boundary system of his or her own so Susan will develop one to protect her.

One of the marks of a functional family is that the children are protected—not overprotected or underprotected, but protected from abusive behaviors while being assisted in constructing strong but flexible boundaries. Susan grows up watching complete boundary systems being modeled, so that she develops one of her own that enables her to be vulnerable to other people when appropriate but also gives her protection against abuse by other adults.

The boundary system also keeps Susan from offending other people. Susan's parents teach her that she can impact other people either positively or negatively. She learns to be sensitive and appropriate when sharing her reality and learns that, just as she has a right to have her reality protected, so does everyone else.

A CHILD IS IMPERFECT

It is absolutely vital to take the characteristic of a child's imperfection into consideration. Children are fallible—they make mistakes all the time as they learn and grow. They are even more imperfect than adults. They haven't had the time and experience in living to know how to confront some of their imperfections and do things more appropriately.

But I want to emphasize this: *in a functional family the members know that EVERYBODY is imperfect.* It's the nature of a human being to be imperfect. As I tell patients, *"Everybody's* poop smells."

HOW A FUNCTIONAL FAMILY SUPPORTS A CHILD'S IMPERFECTION

In a functional family everyone knows that nobody in it is perfect, especially the parents. Functional parents accept the fact that they make mistakes and do not set themselves up as the god and goddess of the family. They know that they must be accountable for actions that are not appropriate. So when parents fail (as they will because they are imperfect) and this failure affects one or more of the children in an adverse way, the parents make amends to the children for what has happened—just as functional adults would make amends to other adults they have affected adversely. I find it necessary to admit mistakes, apologize, and make restitution to my children from time to time. The parents model the fact that people's imperfection is universal and that's okay, and they also expect the children to be imperfect too. So when the children make mistakes or hurt others, they're also taught how to make amends.

For example, I remember a particular incident when one of my sons physically offended his brother. I discussed with the one who committed the offense the fact that hitting, kicking, and other abusive behavior was not acceptable in our family, at the same time supporting him so that he knew that he was a valued member of the family. Next I explained to him that he owed amends to his brother for his behavior and that he should consider making a commitment to himself to stop this physically offensive behavior. He wasn't ready to apologize, but I let him have the time he needed to make the decision to do it. He eventually made amends and has been working on developing his physical boundaries to keep himself from being physically offensive.

Functional parents also have to be observant enough to avoid asking a child to make amends when restitution isn't owed, making sure that the child truly owes an apology. Sometimes the child feels as though he or she hasn't offended the other child and that the parent has misunderstood exactly what has happened. And since all children are manipulative at times, the "offended" child could have misrepresented what happened so that no amends are in order after all.

For example, little Jody is somewhat withdrawn and reserved, and her sister, Tracy, very outgoing and aggressive. When Jody is angry at Tracy, she may not be able to express it directly, but she does express it—in a more indirect covert way, such as "forgetting" where she put the toy she had borrowed from Tracy. She knows that when she does this, Tracy becomes emotionally overwhelmed and goes into a temper tantrum. When Tracy flies off the handle, she attacks Jody, shouting, "You'd better give me back my teddy bear or else!" and hitting her on the arm. Then withdrawn, shy little Jody just stands there with an offended, innocent, wounded look. It is necessary for their parents to know each child well enough to at least check out both children's behavior. If Tracy says, "No, I won't say I'm sorry; Jody started it," the functional parent pays attention to that. When the full story is out, the parents have them both make amends to one another where necessary. Tracy is guided into more acceptable ways of expressing anger than shouting and hitting, and Jody is taught that hiding or "losing" another person's belongings on purpose can be as improper a way to express anger as hitting him or her.

I do not pretend that this is an easy issue when we are dealing with real, live, imperfect children, but I am saying that the *process* of trying to deal fairly and directly with the issue of children's imperfections and the importance of making amends will *in itself* be functional, even though no parent can do it perfectly.

In addition to learning about dealing with their own and others' imperfections, Jody and Tracy are taught how to follow the rules and what to do if they don't. But "who they are" is not attacked when they break the rules, and the message to the children is, despite their imperfect behavior, they are wonderful, precious people. The issue of their worth is never up for debate at all and they are not shamed inordinately because of their imperfection.

It's not that they don't have to follow the rules—of course they are held accountable. If Jody loses Tracy's toy, she is taught how to look for it or to replace it if she can't find it. If she spills her milk, she is taught how to clean it up. If Tracy becomes exasperated and angry at her sister, she is taught how to express her anger without hitting. If she breaks the neighbor's window playing softball, she is taught to apologize and to replace it. In these ways, Jody and Tracy learn to become self-esteeming adults who can embrace their own imperfection and still experience their preciousness from within. They know without any internal debate that they are wonderful human beings—fallible but wonderful.

I think live modeling of dealing with imperfection properly is extremely important, because it seems that only when parents recognize their own imperfections as adults, embrace those imperfections, and demonstrate culpability and the vulnerability of making amends to a child and to other adults in the family does the child learn to be accountable and spiritual as an adult. I mention the child's learning to be spiritual because only if nobody is god or goddess of the family is there much room in the child's life for spirituality and a Higher Power beyond the family. By being accountable for imperfections and relying on a Higher Power for help with these imperfections, parents point the way to a Higher Power for their children. When parents cannot admit their mistakes and be accountable for them, they assume the role of Higher Power for the child, blocking the way to a true Higher Power.

A CHILD IS DEPENDENT (NEEDY AND WANTING)

Children have to rely on other people to get their primary survival needs met. They also need others to satisfy their wants. To keep things simple I have chosen to deal only with certain fundamental dependency needs:

Food	Physical nurturing
Clothing	Emotional nurturing (time, attention
Shelter	and direction)
Medical/	Sexual information and guidance
dental care	Financial information and guidance

All of these elements are important parts of every person's dependency needs. A functional family provides for these needs, and as the children grow older the parents teach them how to meet these needs for themselves. The first five are self-evident, but I want to discuss emotional nurturing, sexual information and guidance, and financial information and guidance in more detail.

I believe the need for emotional nurturing is perhaps the most important one children have, once the basic needs of food, clothing, shelter, and medical/dental attention are provided. The need for emotional nurturing is the need all children have for time and attention from others so that they know they matter and they feel "heard" and visible. This need also includes the requirement for two kinds of information: first about who they are, and second, about how to do things—anything that needs doing in life (e.g. how to make friends, dress, keep clean, be a male or female).

Children who receive enough emotional nurturing develop a sense of who they are, an inner sense of identity. This comes about in two ways. First, children become who *the parent tells them they are* by the parent's words and actions toward the child. Second, children also get a sense of identity by observing and noticing the parent and by *the parent telling the children who the parent is.*

For example, a mother may often say, "I believe that telling the truth is always best, no matter how hard it is to do." And the children remember that she has told the truth at times when it was difficult. She has told them what she believes and she follows through with her behavior often. Her children absorb this value for themselves.

Sexual information and guidance is also an important need children have. Primarily they need suppport and information about their own physical and emotional sexual development. Children need to be in a family environment in which they can explore and learn about themselves and the sexual parts of their bodies. For instance, children develop sexually when they learn such things as the fact that touching certain areas of their bodies is pleasurable. It's very important that they be allowed to develop sexually in a moderate way without being inordinately shamed by anyone. They also need information about what sexual development is.

Children also need to learn about the value of money: how to work for it, how to pay for things, how to save it, spend it, invest it. At some time, I believe children should have a checking account. I also think children need to be included in some family financial decisions. For example, the parents might call a "family meeting" with the children and say something like, "we're going to go on vacation next month. We have this much money and this meeting is to discuss how we're going to manage it."

Children are born with a figurative "Skills for Living" manual that is full of blank pages. They learn about basic being and doing by direct hands-on exchange and specific communication between them and their parents.

We learn what "wants" bring us joy in life by a trial-and-error method. Children develop wants for nonsurvival things in life such as toys, ice cream, certain kinds of shoes to wear to school, and so on. But when the wants are granted, the children learn whether they really were important wants or not; they can tell by the amount of pleasure or satisfaction they experience when their want is granted. And so they develop preferences for certain brands of soft drinks, breakfast cereals, clothing, movies, and so on. And later they apply this procedure to big wants that may change their whole lives and take them in a different direction—wants regarding career, marriage, parenthood, and so on.

HOW A FUNCTIONAL FAMILY MEETS A CHILD'S NEEDS AND WANTS

When Johnny, born into a functional family, has needs or wants, his parents not only respond, but they anticipate his basic needs and are ready to meet them, especially when Johnny is very young. As he gets older the parents' vigilance can be reduced. And as Johnny learns to talk about his neediness and wanting, his parents don't have to be watching so closely, because Johnny will tell them what he needs or wants.

This family environment fosters interdependent adults who now can recognize their own neediness and wanting, respond to it, and take care of it; when the need or want requires help from others, they can ask for help from safe, appropriate people.

Two things happen in a functional family. First of all, the adults are able to identify their own needs and wants. Second, they also know when a legitimate need or want that can't be taken care of by themselves comes up, and they can ask other safe people to help them meet that need or want. This mutual meeting of needs and wants is called interdependence.

For example, I can't hug myself very well. It usually satisfies my need for physical nurturing only when someone else hugs me. Even soaking in a hot bubble bath doesn't take care of the need to be hugged. It's much nicer and more satisfying if my husband or a friend gives me a hug. When I know I need one, I ask.

A CHILD IS IMMATURE

Children pick their noses in the supermarket, swear at their brothers or sisters in front of the priest, rabbi, or the minister who's come to visit, and argue and talk loudly in quiet and formal restaurants. They fight in the back seat during a long trip across the state and they have to go to the bathroom right after you've passed the last gas station for the next hundred miles. A parent who is surprised, angered, or concerned that his or her eight-year-old son "acts like a child" is discounting this basic natural characteristic of immaturity.

HOW A FUNCTIONAL FAMILY SUPPORTS A CHILD'S IMMATURITY

Functional families recognize this immaturity as being natural. Functional parents or caregivers know what to expect at each age level from babies to toddlers up through teenagers and allow children to be children; they do not expect them to be perfect little adults. They do not expect a child to act more mature than his or her age, having to behave and bear responsibility in ways suitable for an older child, nor do they indulge behavior that is clearly suitable for a younger one. When a child is behaving in a way that is clearly "below" his or her age level, the parents functionally assist the child back into acting his or her own age.

If eight-year-old Janie throws a temper tantrum in the middle of the living room floor, her parents don't beat her or verbally attack her for it. They confront the outbreak, intervene, and assist Janie in finding a resolution for her problem. One of them approaches Janie and says something like, "Tell me what's going on with you that you need to lie in the middle of the floor and scream and cry and raise all this ruckus?" Her anger and behavior are not ignored, and Janie is assisted back into acting her age.

I am generally amazed at how well my children respond to this approach. They do *not* respond to my attacking them and telling them, "Stop that *stupid, childish* behavior!" But when I say, "Tell me what's going on with you," it's amazing how all the squabbling stops. I believe that's really what they're looking for.

In a functional family, Janie will be assisted in acting her age but she will not be asked to act older than she is. Her parents do not expect that when she has a problem, she will come to them without crying, sit down, and explain what is troubling her in a rational, articulate manner. She gets to act her age. That's how she gets to have a childhood.

But what happens when these five natural characteristics of all children are exposed to dysfunctional parenting? And how do the attributes get diverted away from mature adult characteristics to the symptoms of codependence?

CHAPTER 5

A Precious Child
in a Dysfunctional Family

Our society often exhibits many unconscious "antichild" cultural values, and even those of us who consider ourselves good parents often behave dysfunctionally toward our children, even as we tell them that what we're doing is "in their best interest."

In looking over our own histories and attempting to get them straight as recovering codependents, we may have to change our minds about some of our own inherited cultural values concerning what is acceptable and unacceptable parenting.

The three attributes of children that I mentioned in the previous chapter, self-centeredness, endless energy, and adaptability, are part of every child's equipment for going through the maturation process of childhood. In dysfunctional families, these three vital tools are used against the children. Dysfunctional parents often attack children, telling them they are abnormal to be self-centered. Dysfunctional parents want their children centered on the parents, so the parents can get their own needs met. And yet it is essential that children have a healthy self-centeredness if they are to develop in a functional way. And when children struggle to adapt into what the parents want, their healthy development is retarded.

The process of abuse depletes the energy children must have to do the work of growing up. When a child is not allowed to be his or her authentic self, the healthy ability to adapt and change is misdirected, and the child is forced to begin the enormous adaptation process into codependence.

As adults we no longer have the self-centeredness, boundless energy, and adaptability we had in childhood. This is true for all adults, but in functional adults these attributes have done their work in the normal growing-up process and are simply not needed as much anymore.

Recovery from codependence is a lot like a growing up process— we must learn to do the things our dysfunctional parents did not teach us to do: appropriately esteem ourselves, set functional boundaries, be aware of and acknowledge our reality, take care of our adult needs and wants, and experience our reality moderately. It takes healthy self-centeredness to esteem ourselves and become aware of our reality, yet when we begin to develop some self-centeredness we may get attacked by others in our life who may interpret it as "selfishness." It takes tremendous energy to set functional boundaries and take care of our needs and wants, but we may notice that we just don't have all that energy any more. And it takes adaptability to change our old patterns of codependence and learn new ways of living in action for ourselves, yet we may find that we have great difficulty changing our ways of thinking and expressing feelings. Since the childhood attributes of self-centeredness, abundant energy, and adaptability have diminished, we are not able to apply them to our present growing-up endeavors, making recovery from codependence more difficult.

In addition to misdirecting these three characteristics, dysfunctional caregivers do not respond appropriately to children's five natural attributes of value, vulnerability, imperfection, dependency, and immaturity. Instead, these caregivers either ignore or attack children for the very essence of who they are, creating an intense experience of shame in the children. Inordinate shaming happens to children when they lose contact with the sense that they are adequate and have value from within, even when making mistakes, having needs, or being immature.

For example, five-year-old Paul makes a mistake at the company picnic and spills his Coke on someone's shoe. His father, Sam, bases his own self-esteem on Paul's behavior in public. Sam feels ashamed because Paul is being imperfect, so he yells at Paul, telling him how stupid, dumb, and worthless he is because he spilled his drink. Sam believes he is using acceptable parenting techniques to teach Paul to be more careful about making mistakes in public, so that Paul will be a better citizen of society when he becomes an adult.

But afterward, little Paul emotionally collapses, feels intense shame, and loses contact with any sense of self-value. Instead of being taught how to apologize for his mistake, Paul identifies himself with his father's shame: "If Dad is so ashamed and angry, I must be pretty crummy."

THE LINK BETWEEN A CHILD'S NATURAL CHARACTERISTICS AND THE SYMPTOMS OF CODEPENDENCE

Children are naturally innocent, inexperienced, naive, and believe that their caregiver can "do no wrong." But in fact caregivers often attack or abuse children for having the normal traits of imperfection, dependency, and immaturity. As a result the children lose their own sense of value (since they can't see that the fault might lie with the caregivers). Also the fact that abuse is occurring means the parents aren't demonstrating boundaries, so the children don't develop their own boundary systems properly.

When the caregivers ignore or attack children's natural characteristics, children develop dysfunctional survival traits to keep from feeling crazy and yet still maintain the belief that the caregivers are always right. They adapt and reshape their mental world to keep from being devastated by the feelings of worthlessness and shame generated in them by the abuse. The dysfunctional survival traits that their natural characteristics are warped into become the core symptoms of codependence when the children become adults. *And I believe that is how codependence is set up.* Chart II shows the specific survival traits that turn into symptoms of codependence when the child becomes an adult.

CHART II: The Effect of Dysfunctional Parenting on the Natural Characteristics of a Child

Natural Characteristics of a Child	when abused become	Dysfunctional Survival Traits	that become	Core Symptoms of Codependence
Valuable		Less-than or Better-than		Difficulty experiencing appropriate levels of self-esteem
Vulnerable		Too vulnerable or Invulnerable		Difficulty setting functional boundaries
Imperfect		Bad/Rebellious or Good/perfect		Difficulty owning and expressing one's own reality and imperfection
Dependent: needing, wanting		Too dependent or Antidependent Needless/Wantless		Difficulty taking care of one's adult needs and wants
Immature		Extremely Immature (Chaotic) or Overmature (Controlling)		Difficulty experiencing and expressing one's reality moderately

A CHILD'S VALUE IN A DYSFUNCTIONAL FAMILY

A dysfunctional family is unable to support the value of the children. The message to them as they are being natural (vulnerable, imperfect, dependent, and immature) is, "There is something wrong with you. Shape up. The fact that you're not being a perfect little person means that you're inadequate and worth less than the rest of us because we don't act like little kids. This is *your* problem."

Or, "Because you need me to do so much for you means I'm better than you are. You better fix yourself!" And the family tries to force the children into doing things perfectly or at least the way the family wants the children to do them. They often put pressure on children to deny their own dependency needs and wants so as not to bother the parents. And they do not help the children act their own age, either pushing them to act older or allowing them to act younger.

Because of these attitudes, the children may never sense their inherent worth, may feel worth less than others (especially major caregivers and later other authority figures). They may learn to esteem themselves based on the perceived quality of their "doing" or performance, not their existence. Such children believe that esteem will come from external things, such as how good their grades are, how many honors they can win (in athletics or scholarship), whom they date, what they wear, how pretty or handsome they are, the approval of others for their accomplishments or behavior and so on. This is other-esteem based on things outside the self.

In some children low self-esteem does not seem to show. Instead they appear to be very arrogant and grandiose. This often comes from a family system that teaches the children to be contemptuous of other people or perhaps from observing a parent who puts himself or herself above others. "Never forget, we are Wilsons (or Feldmans or McAdams or whoever). We are better than anybody else." So even though children in this situation may be criticized and inordinately shamed by the parents, they wind up learning to gather other-esteem by putting themselves above other people to cover their own feelings of worthlessness. Such people act out of the "better-than," arrogant, and grandiose survival trait on Chart II.

Some children develop a "better-than" trait when their families treat them as if they are actually of more value than the other children in the family, and perhaps of more value than the parents. Such children are placed on a pedestal, imperfection is minimized or ignored, and they are not taught that everyone has equal value.

These children *do not* experience any low self-worth that they must disguise by *acting* arrogant. They truly believe they *are* better. This empowering form of abuse is very hard to treat and can lead to disastrous personal relationships.

Billy, who was born into a dysfunctional family, is told by his mother that it's bedtime. He announces, "I don't want to go to bed." His mother grabs him by the arm, shakes him, and tries to physically strong-arm him into the bedroom screaming, "Don't talk to me that way! It's time to go to bed and I don't care about what you want or don't want." This mother's response indicates that she has no respect for the fact that Billy has value even when he doesn't want to go to bed. The message is that it is not okay with Billy's mother for him to have his honest feelings. And Billy develops the belief that he has little or no value when he expresses his distress about something he doesn't want to do.

Billy's mother also says, "Okay, because you wouldn't go to bed when I told you to, you don't get to go play outside for a week." These are exaggerated consequences, ones not based on the fact that he didn't get enough sleep for one night, but on some other criteria that are out of proportion to Billy's behavior.

Billy becomes sensitive to the idea that his behavior dictates his worth to his parents, and he believes who he *is* (a child who doesn't want to go to bed) is worthless. He believes that he is "no good" because he couldn't "want" to go to bed when he was told to. Also, he sees eventually that when he can cheerfully and promptly go to bed (even if he has to hide his distress and pretend to be cheerful), he apparently has value and worth (though in fact this is other-esteem based on doing rather than being). His own reality of distress is not acknowledged and Billy is taught other-esteem. Billy may develop the characteristic survival trait of working very hard at pleasing people because he does not know how to esteem himself.

CODEPENDENT ADULT CHARACTERISTIC

When a child's value is exposed to either shaming or empowering dysfunctional parenting, the resulting survival trait is one of two extremes: he or she either feels "less than" other people or has an attitude of being better than others. Either of these traits develops into the adult core symptom of difficulty experiencing appropriate levels of self-esteem. *Both* the low self-esteem response and the arrogant, grandiose response to the dysfunctional parenting stem from the *same problem*: lack of awareness of one's own value.

Some people experience this symptom at only one end of the scale, either the low or nonexistent self-esteem position or the better-than, arrogant position, but others swing back and forth between the two.

CHILD'S VULNERABILITY
IN A DYSFUNCTIONAL FAMILY

Children develop whatever boundary system the parents have. If a parent is dysfunctional and doesn't have an adequately developed boundary system, the children develop no boundaries or damaged ones—they become "too vulnerable." They walk into the face of danger with no idea that the danger even exists. They are too trusting and continue to expose themselves to parents, other caregivers, and even strangers who, acting without boundaries themselves, abuse them. When children mimic the walls they see their parents using, they develop the trait of being invulnerable. Such children protect themselves from abuse by withdrawing behind a wall of fear or silence or aggressively throwing up walls of anger or words.

A dysfunctional family abuses children's vulnerability by failing to protect them and failing to teach them how to avoid offending others. Since children are naturally vulnerable, they have not developed their own boundaries with which they will later protect themselves and keep from being offensive to others.

For example, one day ten-year-old Patsy decided to take a short cut home from the school bus stop through a neighbor's yard, and along the way she stepped on some flowers. The yard owner, Mr. Henley, rushed out of his house with a garden rake, yelling "Get out of here, little girl, before I beat the tar out of you!" Patsy ran frantically home in tears and told her mother what Mr. Henley had done. Patsy's mother gave her a verbal tongue-lashing, telling her she deserved what she got because she stepped in Mr. Henley's flower bed. In effect, both Mr. Henley and Patsy's mother dealt with Patsy's imperfection inappropriately.

While Patsy is clearly in the wrong and has made a mistake, she does not deserve to be threatened with a beating by a dangerous implement nor screamed at. Her own lack of boundaries led her to think it was acceptable to walk through the neighbor's yard and her carelessness led her to damaging the flowers. Patsy needs to be taught to respect the property of others. But her parents also need to defend Patsy against Mr. Henley's abusive response to Patsy's mistake. First, they need *not* tell Patsy she deserved the threats and second, they might consider going with Patsy to Mr. Henley's house and helping her apologize to him, saying that they will teach Patsy to stay out of his yard, but also that they do not approve of his threatening their child with a rake and screaming at her. They accompany their child to do this in order to protect her from any possible additional abusive behavior on Mr. Henley's part.

CODEPENDENT ADULT CHARACTERISTIC

When children's *vulnerability* is exposed to a dysfunctional family, they grow up with whatever dysfunctional boundary system the parents have. For instance, if the parents have nonexistent boundaries or damaged ones, the children are too vulnerable. As an adult, the person continues to feel too vulnerable and also operates with nonexistent or damaged boundaries. This adult cannot properly protect himself or herself in relationships, nor prevent himself or herself from being offensive to others.

If the parents used a wall of any kind, the children also start using the same kind of wall, becoming invulnerable. When these invulnerable children become adult codependents, they have learned to use walls for protection instead of healthy boundaries. These adults protect themselves from abuse from others but may abuse others with their walls. They are also isolated and alone and suffer from lack of intimacy that healthy relationships with others would provide.

If one parent had nonexistent or damaged boundaries and the other used walls, the children may swing from being too vulnerable to being invulnerable. As adult codependents, such people continue to swing from nonexistent or damaged boundaries to walls, from being too vulnerable to being invulnerable, without finding a comfortable way to relate to people. Any of these three responses leads to dysfunctional adult behavior and relationships.

A CHILD'S RIGHT TO BE IMPERFECT
IN A DYSFUNCTIONAL FAMILY

Dysfunctional families do not recognize and respect the fact that children, like everyone else, are imperfect. Children may be attacked for their imperfection and given the message that it is abnormal to be imperfect. They have two choices in responding to this parental demand for perfection. They can try to meet the demand, complying and becoming good and perfectionistic little people. Or the children can be overwhelmed by the parent's impossible demands and rebel, refusing to cooperate and actually working to be the opposite of what the parents are demanding. These children are labeled "rebellious" or "bad" by the parents.

On the other hand, children's imperfection may be ignored and they never learn that they have any imperfection or that they need to be responsible and accountable when their imperfect behavior affects other people in an adverse way. These children also are seen by society as "rebellious" and "spoiled." They do not know how to notice when their imperfection hurts or inconveniences others so that they can be accountable for the part of their imperfection that is abusive.

Four-year-old Mary spills her milk because four-year-olds aren't fully coordinated and often spill things. But her mother attacks her, saying "Shame on you for spilling the milk. You're a bad little girl. Good girls don't spill their milk. Don't ever do that again." Mary's mother is attacking what is normal and imperfect for Mary at her age and demanding that Mary do something that is unnatural for her at age four. If Mary is cooperative, she will strain to never spill things and even try to do everything else perfectly. If Mary is overwhelmed by the demand, she may rebel and deliberately spill things, working against what her mother is demanding of her.

Kerry is a twelve-year-old child in a dysfunctional family. When he was clumsy and tripped on the stairs, knocking over a potted plant, his mother shouted, "Oops, there goes elephant-foot!" and tells him that good boys don't wreck the house just by walking through it. When he got mad at his brother, he shouted profanity at him and physically shoved him out of his room so hard that his brother fell backwards on the floor. His father beat him with a belt without asking what the brother had done to provoke Kerry. Of course Kerry needs to be taught how to express his anger in a way that doesn't hurt anyone. But the mother's verbal name-calling and exaggerated demand that Kerry be "good" and not "wreck the house" was shaming to Kerry and did not take into account the normal clumsiness of being twelve. And the father's beating was an act of physical abuse that did very little to help Kerry and his brother learn how to settle their disagreements. His parents used his imperfection as occasions for him to be shamed and abused.

Kerry, as an adult trying to get his history straight, reported to me that he had suffered a lot of physical abuse. But then I asked him, "Why did you get physically abused? Why did your dad take his belt off and beat you like that? What had you done?"

He shook his head and said, "I don't know."

I see many patients who don't know why they were abused, and I usually tell them what I told Kerry. "It may be that you were just acting like a kid and that's why you can't remember."

If people can recall specific punishment as children, most of them can remember the reason: perhaps they burned down the tree in the back yard and got a whipping for it. The reason for the whipping was clear, even if it was abusive. Children also just spill milk, scream in their bedroom, call their brother or sister names, and fight. But when they get punished for things like *this*, they can seldom remember as adult what happened or why they got punished. That's because the parents didn't understand that children are imperfect and attacked and punished them for simply being what they were. Kerry, like other children who experience this, grew up being a perfectionist.

On the other hand, in some dysfunctional family systems, when children demonstrate imperfection, they are not held accountable for the consequences at all. They are neither punished nor given any information about what to do instead, no instruction about how to do things better. These children wind up being rebellious, or "bad."

Parents who treat their children's imperfection dysfunctionally often do not acknowledge their *own* imperfection either. My clinical experience indicates that such parents usually do not have a good working concept of spirituality, even though they might appear to be extremely religious. Practical spirituality is about a relationship with a Power who is higher than any person in the family—including the parents. We will look more closely at this notion of spirituality in Part Three.

CODEPENDENT ADULT CHARACTERISTIC

Many children who were attacked for making mistakes become perfectionist adults who also are very controlling. On the other hand, children who did not have to be accountable for mistakes or who gave up trying to be perfect and resisted their parents demands may well become rebellious adult codependents and exhibit little and sometimes no control over themselves. Adults who were raised as perfectionists or "spoiled" rebels have difficulty owning and expressing their own reality and imperfection. These adults are not now able to know themselves realistically as normally imperfect human beings without great fear, pain, or anger attached to that knowledge. Thus it becomes difficult to acknowledge what we think, feel, did, or look like because the emotional reaction to any imperfection is so painful. The fear of failure on any test of ability is especially intense for such codependents.

A CHILD'S DEPENDENCY IN A DYSFUNCTIONAL FAMILY

Children depend on their caregivers to meet all their needs and wants at first, and then, in functional families, gradually learn from the caregivers how to meet their own needs and wants, and how to ask for help from appropriate others when necessary without shame or guilt. When a child's state of dependence is parented in a dysfunctional manner, the child becomes either too dependent, feeling too needy and too wanting, or becomes antidependent, or needless and wantless.

There are three primary abuse situations most children face with dysfunctional parents concerning their needs and wants: (1) having the parent enmesh with and always take care of everything, never letting the children do anything for themselves, (2) being attacked, or (3) being ignored.

In the first case, when the parent takes care of everything, never letting the children learn to do for themselves, the children become too dependent simply because they lack skill in self-care and expect others to take care of them. For example, eight-year-old David is hungry and he asks to eat. His mother automatically makes him a sandwich but never bothers to show David how to make the sandwich so that when he's hungry he can make one for himself. She continues to make sandwiches for him when he's twelve and when he's sixteen and he never learns how to make a sandwich because his mother always does it for him.

In the second case, when children have a need, the parents attack them and they learn that it is unsafe to express a need or a want. Sammy is hungry and asks to eat. His mother tells him, "You're a selfish pig, Sammy. It's too early to eat now and you're asking too much of me to stop ironing and fix you something to eat. You'll just have to wait for dinner like everyone else." But Sammy is still hungry and she does not fix him anything, so he goes ahead and struggles through the sandwich making process, learning that it isn't safe to ask anyone to make a sandwich. "I guess I'll just have to do it myself when I get hungry."

In the third case, the parents ignore practically all needs and wants of the children almost from birth. When little Sherry was hungry and said so, her mother often did not respond at all. Instead of learning to make a sandwich, she became numb to her awareness of her hunger.

CODEPENDENT ADULT CHARACTERISTIC

Whether too dependent, antidependent, or needless and wantless, adult codependents experience the symptom of having difficulty acknowledging and taking care of their own adult needs and wants.

Too-dependent adults, who never learned how to meet their own needs and wants, are aware of them but spend a lot of energy trying to get somebody else to meet them through whining or some other form of manipulation. For example, the now-adult David knows when he is hungry but he expects his wife to fix food for him, and complains if dinner is late. When his wife left town for a week to take care of their daughter and her new baby, she filled the freezer with casseroles and left detailed written instructions on how to thaw them, knowing that David couldn't fix anything for himself. But David often went to the nearby cafeteria for dinner, since even thawing a casserole seemed overwhelming to him.

Antidependent adults who learned that asking for help in meeting a need or want is likely to invite abuse, have an awareness of their needs and wants and meet the ones they can fairly well. But they have an inability to ask others for help with regard to needs or wants that they don't know how to meet. An antidependent codependent would rather go with the need unmet than have to ask for help.

For example, little Sammy is now an adult who rarely asks anyone for anything and feels a great deal of shame when he cannot do something for himself and has to ask. When he was twenty-eight, he had a skiing accident and spent some time in a hospital room with his leg in traction. One day he woke up from a nap very thirsty from the pain medication and noticed that his water pitcher was empty. He could not get out of bed to fill it, so he waited for a nurse to walk in, notice the pitcher, and fill it up. When a nurse did walk in to check on him, he started to tell her he needed water but got embarrassed and changed his mind. The nurse didn't notice that his water pitcher was empty and left. He waited another hour, at which time his dinner tray arrived and the attendant refilled the water pitcher. He had been miserable from thirst for two hours, but he would rather have been thirsty than ask someone to fill the water pitcher.

The needless and wantless adult is one whose needs and wants were almost completely ignored in childhood. These people have little or no awareness that their needs or wants even exist. For example, as an adult Sherry has lost most of her awareness of her needs for food, clothing, shelter, medical and dental attention, physical nurturing, emotional nurturing, and so forth, just as her mother has shown no awareness of Sherry's needs for these things. As a result, Sherry doesn't eat proper food, has inadequate clothing, toothaches, and a barren personal life because she is not aware of her needs and consequently doesn't do anything to meet them.

Another example is that of Sally, who is unaware of her need for physical nurturing. Sally does not know that she needs to be physically touched through hugs, hand-holding, and so on. But since this is a basic human need, the deprivation she suffers will affect her ability to sustain functional relationships.

One way Sally may act is to inappropriately touch and smother other people, consciously believing she is meeting *their* need for physical touch, when actually she is meeting her own unfelt need in an indirect way. In so doing she may not sense that others may find the physical contact inappropriate, leading them to back off from her.

At the other extreme Sally may not be physically demonstrative at all, neither giving hugs or touches nor receiving them. People in a relationship with her feel awkward about touching or hugging her, and they also long for physical demonstrations of affection from the "needless" one. Unfortunately needless/wantless codependents do not even know these demonstrations are needed and wanted by those close to them.

A CHILD'S IMMATURITY IN A DYSFUNCTIONAL FAMILY

When immature children are exposed to dysfunctional parenting, they become either chaotic or controlling. A dysfunctional family expects children to act more mature than they could possibly be, or indulges and allows them to behave immaturely beneath their age level.

Sara and Donna are sisters being raised in a dysfunctional family. Sarah was required to be more mature than she could possibly be. At age four her parents expected her to act like she was eight or nine, sitting quietly through an entire church service and behaving properly in restaurants. When Sarah was eight she began to have to babysit her younger sister, Donna, for several hours in the afternoons while her mother ran errands. Donna was three when this pattern began, and Sarah often felt overwhelmed with fear that Donna might get hurt because Sarah was not watching her closely enough. She also knew if Donna got into trouble she too would be punished. And she was angry about having to stay in the house after school watching Donna instead of riding her bicycle with the other girls her age. Sarah became a very bossy, nosy, resentful older sister. As she was pushed to older age levels, she never had a chance to experience her own childhood.

On the other hand, Sarah's younger sister, Donna, was indulged and allowed to act much younger than was appropriate for her age. When she, at age eight, had a temper tantrum like a two-year-old, it was not confronted. It was tolerated and even catered to. Donna got so much attention, sympathy, and comfort from throwing her temper tantrums that she never learned what was expected of her at age eight and later.

In some cases, children can experience both of these opposite dysfunctional treatments at different times or from different parents.

CODEPENDENT ADULT CHARACTERISTIC

In adulthood, either of the effects of mishandled childhood immaturity (being chaotic or being controlling) results in difficulty experiencing and expressing one's reality in moderation. As a codependent adult, Sarah will probably become an overmature, controlling person. Donna will probably remain immature and her adult life and relationships will be chaotic. Neither sister had the chance to act her age when growing up; they received too little time, attention, and direction concerning how to live appropriately.

CHAPTER 6

The Emotional Damage of Abuse

Dysfunctional parenting damages us in numerous ways. It may scar our bodies or render them unhealthy, overweight, or underweight; it may thwart our ability to be sexually healthy; it skews our thinking; it often distorts our spiritual lives; and it creates bizarre or erratic behavior. But I believe it is the emotional damage we suffer that most profoundly sabotages our lives as adult codependents. Our emotions are often either overwhelming and seemingly irrational or we are so cut off from our feelings that we are emotionally numb. Understanding the nature of this emotional damage is, for me, the key to understanding how codependence works in adults.

Feeling healthy emotions is a positive experience. There is absolutely nothing wrong with any of our emotions, as long as they are expressed in a healthy, functional way and not an abusive one. As part of the equipment we need to live life fully and functionally, each of our emotions has a specific purpose.

Anger gives us the strength we need to do what is necessary to take care of ourselves. Anger enables us to assert ourselves and be who we are. We can use healthy anger to our own best interest by facing it and expressing it in nonabusive ways (either to ourselves or others).

Fear helps us protect ourselves. When we feel fear, we become alert to the possibility of danger in our environment from which we need to protect ourselves. Healthy fear keeps us from getting into situations and relationships that would not be in our own best interest.

Pain motivates us to grow toward increasing maturity. Normal healthy lives are full of pain-producing problems, and feeling the pain produces growth. Many of us were told in our family of origin that mature people didn't have problems or pain and so when we did have both, we thought something was wrong with us.

Because of life's routine problems and difficulties we will all be in pain from time to time. A functional person uses pain as a means to work through problems, heal from their effects, gain the wisdom that comes our of painful situations, and continue in the maturing process. Repressing the pain and not facing it or medicating it in some way keeps us injured and immature.

Guilt is a healthy warning system telling us we have transgressed a value we consider to be important. Feeling guilt helps us change our behavior and get back to living up to our values.

Shame gives us a sense of humility that lets us know we are not the Higher Power. Healthy shame reminds us that we are fallible, and that we need to learn to be accountable and responsible. Shame also helps us to correct our areas of fallibility that impact others and society adversely. This process helps us to accept the rest of our imperfection as part of our normal, healthy humanity. We can also relate to a Higher Power in a healthy way that is necessary to live as a responsible, mature adult. We experience shame whenever we notice ourselves making a mistake or being imperfect.

Although everybody is imperfect, children are more imperfect than adults because they haven't yet been taught to correct some of their imperfection so they can be more socially appropriate. A parent responds to a child's fallibility by correcting the very important areas which, if not corrected, will negatively affect the child or society.

Healthy shame does not appear to me to be generated naturally from within as are anger, pain, fear, and joy. I think shame is passed from generation to generation through the process of adults correcting children.

Healthy, supportive, and respectful correction triggers the development of a child's natural shame. Let's say a small boy is picking his nose in the shopping mall and his mother wants to teach him not to do that without shaming him inordinately. She gets close enough to him so he can hear her talking quietly and calmly says, "Stan, we don't pick our noses in public and I want you to stop. Here's a Kleenex. If your nose is bothering you, blow your nose into this Kleenex." This is an approach for a child who is old enough to hear and respond, not one who is too young to understand. Stan may experience embarrassment as this correction develops his own healthy shame.

When caregivers correct a child in a humiliating, coercive, disrespectful way, the child feels not just embarrassed, but less-than, inadequate, and worthless. We shall see how this happens later in this chapter.

A child raised in a family that never corrects the child develops no shame at all—not even healthy shame. I find the feelings of anger, pain, fear, and joy in such a person, but not shame, which is why I believe shame is not generated from within but comes to the child through the process of being corrected by the caregiver. Such shameless children have little or no healthy shame to notify themselves of their own fallibility and usually exhibit arrogance and grandiosity, thinking that everything they do is acceptable. If someone objects to what they do, they believe themselves misunderstood or misinterpreted, or that there is something wrong with the person objecting.

WHAT OUR SOCIETY SAYS ABOUT FEELINGS

Our culture divides our feelings into two kinds: "good" and "bad." Anger, pain, fear, guilt, and shame are labeled bad or negative. Joy we consider good or positive. Unfortunately, this sort of "black or white" categorizing is erroneous and dysfunctional.

One dysfunctional message our culture gives us is that most of the time it's not acceptable to have "bad" feelings listed above. The message to children is that mature, well-controlled, successful adult people stay "rational" at all times, which means staying out of "bad" feelings. By the time one is an adult, the message often is, "If you're really mature, you don't need to have 'bad' feelings."

Paralleling that message is one that says that if a person *does* own and express any such emotions, that person is immature. If the feelings are moderately intense, the person is labelled "emotional" (as opposed to rational). And if the feelings are extremely intense, the person has moved into the realm of craziness. Since one of the major symptoms of codependence is "feeling crazy" because our emotions seem to be almost out of control, we codependents feel a lot of guilt and shame in our culture for being who we are.

Another cultural message is that even if it is acceptable to our family and friends for us to have some feelings, there are still *certain* feelings that we're not to have. For example, in our society, men must not have fear. If a man is afraid, he's a coward. It's acceptable for a woman to be afraid, because she's supposed to be weak and vulnerable. But women must not be angry. If a woman is angry, she's a witch. But a man's anger is his male right; he's just exerting his power.

Pain is not acceptable for either sex. The message is, "You have a right not to have any pain, so take whatever you need to numb it." Since wisdom and maturity come from facing pain and learning from it, I believe we are a nation of very immature people who don't have the willingness to experience the pain that leads to authentic wisdom. We haven't learned how to tolerate pain and deal with it as an agent of positive change.

SHAME AND GUILT

Another emotion regulated by our society is shame. According to our culture, we may feel shame, but *we're not supposed to talk about it*. As a result, many of us are out of touch with the fact that our lives are filled with experiences of shame. This is particularly unfortunate for codependents because, as we shall see in this chapter, codependence is a shame-based illness, and it's hard to get into recovery when the one thing we need to talk about is not supposed to be revealed or discussed. Codependents who have responded to their childhood abuse with an arrogant, grandiose stance have a particularly hard time because they have almost totally repressed their shame or never developed any during childhood.

Shame is an emotion like guilt, pain, or joy, but it is special because it affects our sense of worth by letting us know that we are imperfect and not the Higher Power, forcing us to be accountable for who we are and be in relationship with a power greater than ourselves. For this reason, shame is the primary feeling that influences "who we are."

Shame is extremely powerful. Many people think that anger is the most powerful feeling we experience, but in my opinion shame is. Patients who have become able to identify their own experiences of shame tell me that shame is more powerful than anger for them as well.

Natural shame (that is, healthy shame) tells us that we are imperfect and that we are not God. We experience natural shame as a mild to moderate feeling of embarrassment when we notice ourselves making a mistake or being imperfect—"I'm only human, after all!" The intensity might move from mild to moderate to strong, but it isn't overwhelming. Shame alerts us to the fact that we may be offending someone or ourselves. Shame "notifies" our conscious mind that we have made a mistake, and we need to correct it or to stop doing whatever we're doing, because it's not appropriate.

When we can feel our own natural shame, we get two vital aids for living. First, becoming aware that we are not perfect allows us to be accountable and to relate to other people intimately and not from a superior position. Second, when our own natural shame tells us we are not the Higher Power, this awareness allows us to be spiritual and humble enough to receive help from a Higher Power. Shame is a built-in regulator to keep us from getting too grandiose about our abilities and from forgetting about our status as created beings rather than the Creator. The ability to deal with our own shame allows us to become sensitive and free spiritual beings. In my opinion, being in touch with our own spirituality is crucial to recovery in a Twelve-Step Program. In the first place each of the Twelve Steps is about either accountability or spirituality. But beyond that, authentic spirituality is about being accepted, loved, and valued in a relationship with Ultimate Reality—our value and self-acceptance are experiencially verified as we relate to the Truth itself.

Guilt is an uncomfortable or gnawing feeling in the abdomen about an *action* or *thought* that transgresses our value system, accompanied by a sense of wrongness. Guilt is often confused with natural shame, which is experienced as embarrassment and perhaps a flushed face, accompanied by a sense of fallibility.

For example, I feel guilty and experience that gnawing feeling in my abdomen if I lie to someone, because my value system includes telling the truth. I feel shame or embarrassed if someone notices me tripping while going down the stairs. I did not transgress a value system, I merely made a mistake that people noticed. If someone noticed that I was lying and confronted me about it, I would feel not only guilt for lying but also shame because someone else noticed my imperfection.

A codependent doesn't know how to tell the difference between healthy shame and guilt very well and often thinks it's guilt when it's really shame. But as we saw on page 91, both of these feelings together give us humility and accountability, important tools for living. Each feeling is a vital part of a healthy, functional person's range of emotions. I suggest that whenever you're not sure which you're feeling, ask yourself this question: "Did I break my own rules, or am I just noticing (or is someone else noticing) me making a mistake?"

INDUCED OR CARRIED FEELINGS

When I first started working with patients who had significant childhood abuse experiences, I noticed the presence in them of unusually intense shame and other overwhelming feelings. Victims of child abuse seemed to experience shame, pain, fear, and anger far in excess of that which seemed appropriate for the adult, nonabusive situation. These feelings *had* to somehow be connected to the earlier child abuse experiences themselves. As I listened to the patients' stories, it began to appear as if, as children, they had "picked up" the very strong feelings from their abusers during abuse experiences, as if the abusers were somehow "inducing" the feelings in the children. The children then "carried" these induced feelings into adulthood with them.

I have come to believe that when a caregiver abuses a child, the caregiver is out of touch with his or her own healthy shame. This is probably because the caregiver is in the throes of overwhelming shame carried from his or her own childhood abuse experiences. If the caregiver could feel healthy shame, he or she would stop abusing the child. As a result of being abused by a shame-filled parent out of touch with his or her shame, the child somehow develops a core of shame induced by the parent during abuse.

Electrical circuit theory provides a helpful analogy. Alternating electric current passed through a coil will induce current in a second coil in close proximity to the first coil. In a similar way, intense feelings surging through an abusive caregiver induce the same feelings in the nearby child victim and become a core of feeling reality. This process seems to happen especially with the feeling of shame, but it also happens with anger, fear, and pain.

When people experience feelings, they give off energy that others can sense. I have noticed that when I am standing within eighteen inches of certain people, they don't have to tell me what they are feeling. I can sense their anger, pain, or joy. Our feelings can probably impact ourselves and others more powerfully than any other part of our reality and without our being aware that any impact is taking place.

At any rate, my clinical experience indicates that these powerful feelings are first induced into children during abuse. Later, as adults, these abuse survivors have recurrences of the same feelings they absorbed in childhood but they do not know them as such; instead the feelings appear to manifest themselves as overwhelming emotional reactions to present-day events. The induction of feelings into a child can occur whether the caregiver delivers passive or withdrawing abuse, such as abandonment and neglect, or active, attacking abuse such as physical beating or verbal attacks.

CARRIED FEELING REALITY: AN OVERWHELMING EXPERIENCE

One way to tell the difference between carried feelings and your own healthy ones is that carried feelings are overwhelming while your own, even though they may be intense, are not. When we experience *carried anger*, we rage; when we experience *carried fear*, we have panic attacks and attacks of paranoia; when we experience *carried or induced pain*, we move into hopelessness, profound feelings of depression, and perhaps even thoughts of suicide. *Carried shame* tells us we are "worth less."

Chemically dependent people die from the chemicals if there is no intervention. Codependents die from suicide, "accidents," physical or medical self-neglect, or the dreadful experience of never really living their own lives, which is a form of living death. Depressed codependents do not take care of themselves when symptoms of physical illness appear or get "careless" and have accidents that can be fatal.

Chart III shows healthy versus carried or induced feelings.

CHART III: Experiencing Healthy and Carried Feelings

Experiencing One's Own Feelings	Feeling Reality	Experiencing Induced or Carried Feelings
Feelings of power and energy	Anger	Feelings of rage
A sense of protection and wisdom	Fear	Feelings of panic or paranoia
Awareness of growth and healing	Pain	Feelings of hopelessness and depression
Humility and an awareness of fallibility	Shame	Feelings of being less than others, worth nothing

THE EXPERIENCE OF CARRIED SHAME

I consider shame to be both a gift from God and a legacy of abuse. When it's a gift from God, the experience of our own natural shame makes us aware that we are fallible. But shame as a legacy of abuse has to do with the devastating and crippling experience of carried or induced shame because it is this shame that diminishes our sense of our inherent worth, making us feel less than others.

It's not a matter of just feeling imperfect and accountable (as we do with natural shame). We feel a much deeper experience of "less than." We may feel mortified, worthless, and horrible about ourselves. When we are experiencing induced or carried shame we don't want to see anyone or have anyone see us. We can't look people in the eye or speak to them without agonizing feelings of shame. We sometimes feel "lost" and often "crazy" while engulfed by carried shame experiences.

I call an encounter with carried shame a "shame attack." In a shame attack you may feel as though your body is getting smaller. You may blush, want to disappear, run away, or crawl under your chair. It seems that everyone is looking at you. Feeling nauseated, dizzy, or spacey is also common. You might start talking in a tiny childlike voice. And there is a tendency to "replay the scene" in your mind and let the shame feelings increase the next time through. In general, the experience of a shame attack is a dreadful sense of inadequacy.

HOW FEELINGS GET INDUCED INTO A CHILD

We learn to experience an induced feeling reality as a result of being abused. The principle is this: *Whenever a major caregiver is abusing a child while DENYING or BEING IRRESPONSIBLE WITH his or her feeling reality, the feeling reality is very likely to be induced in the child who becomes overwhelmed by the caregiver's feeling reality.* The only thing that could stop this transference of feelings from happening would be for children to have adequate internal boundary systems; but children's internal boundary systems are not fully developed and they cannot keep from taking on the feelings of the adult offender.

In an abusive home the caregivers repeatedly act irresponsibly with their feelings, or they deny them. These feelings keep shifting to the child and become part of the child's core of feelings.

Shame is the primary feeling passed to the child. I believe this because it is "shameless" to abuse a defenseless child. A shameless person is one who is denying his or her own shame, which passes directly to the child. The child's own shame gives him or her a sense of fallibility, but adding the parent's shame to the child's shame gives the child an overwhelming sense of worthlessness, "badness," and inadequacy.

In any family system, even a functional one, the parents occasionally fail to act in the child's best interest. No parent is perfect and every parent or caregiver is likely to be less than nurturing at times. But in a functional system parents are accountable when they fail to be there for the child. The parents experience their imperfectness — and natural shame — and make amends to the child, relieving the child of the sense of overwhelming shame and worthlessness.

But when the parents in a dysfunctional system repeatedly deny their own feelings of shame, or are irresponsible with their own feelings of shame, the child gets inordinately shamed more and more. The child develops a core of induced shame as a result (which I call a "shame core") that *constantly* tells the child (and later adult) that he or she has less value than other people.

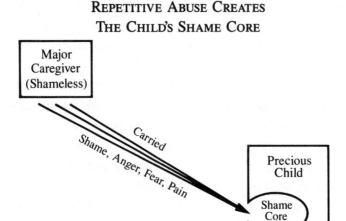

REPETITIVE ABUSE CREATES
THE CHILD'S SHAME CORE

This message, "you have less value than others," forms the basis for the first symptom of codependence, difficulty experiencing appropriate levels of self-esteem, and is, I believe, the heart of codependence. And this is why codependence is called a shame-based disease.

THE EMOTIONAL CONDITION
OF THE ABUSIVE CAREGIVER

Dysfunctional caregivers are shame-based people themselves. They can't *feel* their own natural shame because it's repressed and covered up by the shame core induced in them by their own caregivers. Being controlled by a carried shame core sets people up to be less than nurturing to their own children.

Such caregivers constantly try to gather other-esteem from their environment to counteract the worthless feelings generated by the induced shame core. So when a child makes a mistake in public, for example, the parent has a shame attack about the *child's behavior*, which sets the parent up to be abusive toward the child.

In my opinion, shame-based parents can very rarely be appropriate parents. They will abuse either by direct attack or by neglect and withdrawal.

HOW OTHER FEELINGS CAN BE PASSED DURING ABUSE

Feelings other than shame can be absorbed by the child into the shame core if the caregiver is denying or being irresponsible with them. When little Glenda makes a mistake and spills her milk at the table, Dad flies into a rage. He punishes her at that moment while he is still angry, and screams at her, so Glenda gets a good dose of her father's anger along with the shame. If this were a recurring experience for her, Glenda's therapist may find that Glenda still carries a great deal of anger in her own shame core later in adulthood.

Pain could also be induced into Glenda in the following way. Her mother watches her dad raging at Glenda for spilling the milk. On one level Glenda's mother understands that it's not acceptable for her dad to rage at her. Glenda's mother has a lot of pain and fear of her own, but instead of using these feelings to protect her daughter, she holds them in and is thereby irresponsible with them. If Glenda is near her mother and realizes she isn't going to protect her, Glenda absorbs the fear and pain her mother is being irresponsible with in addition to the anger and shame from her dad. I hope it is becoming apparent why the current exaggerated feelings of codependents are so baffling and "out of proportion" with regard to what is presently going on around them.

I realize there is not way to prove this, but in therapy many codependents report feelings that fit this description. Revealing how both parents were involved in the abuse has proved very helpful.

In another example of transferring pain, a woman continually complains to her daughter, while weeping and wailing, about what a cad the girl's father is and how painful life is. Then unaccountably the mother starts feeling better. But as she does, the daughter begins feeling the pain of her mother's unhappy life. So when she grows up, she carries an irrational pain inside her shame core and has no idea why she hurts all the time. Before she came for therapy she spent much time trying to fix other people's pain, fear, and anger in hopes of quieting those feelings in herself.

Fear might be induced into a child when a parent is fearless about abusing a child. The mother of one of my clients started beating her when she was an infant and continued until she was about age four. She finally stopped only because the family insisted that she stop. When the child grew up and came for therapy, she was terribly frightened much of the time. I finally saw that she had gotten the fear because her mother was out of touch with her own fear of harming her infant daughter during the beatings.

I've noticed that I can induce feelings into my own children. I remember a day when I was at the kitchen sink grinding my teeth because my husband, Pat, had just bought another old car and put it in the yard by our garden. I didn't like it.

One of my sons came in and a few moments later said, "Mom, are you angry?"

"No I'm fine, son," I answered.

He asked me several more times, and each time I told him I wasn't angry. So as I denied my anger, guess who got it? My son. Within ten minutes he was fighting with his brother in the back bedroom, using the anger I wasn't facing. Whenever I am denying my feeling reality, my children will take it on if they're around me.

What I needed to tell him was, "Yes, I'm angry, but it's not about you. I'm angry about the old car out there in the front yard by the garden." I would have acknowledged my feelings and he could have continued playing, having been relieved of worrying about my feelings.

If children are repetitively abused by different people, shame can be passed to them from more than one caregiver. Or in one simple act of abuse a child can be completely overwhelmed by several feelings (as happened to Glenda). If the incidents of abuse are repeated, the shame core gets huge and a codependent adult's feelings can be almost completely dominated by the carried or induced feeling reality. This results in a sense of being crazy and a degree of codependence that is very difficult to treat. Multiple abusers, a high frequency of abuse, and the induction of several feelings at once all complicate the therapist's task of separating skewed feelings and thinking from appropriate ones and adequately treating a codependent.

WHAT GENERATES FEELINGS?

While I realize that there are several models for describing what triggers our emotions, there is one that has been quite helpful in examining a factor that accentuates the damage to our feeling reality. Beside the fact that we now carry feelings induced in us during childhood, the fact that *our emotions are generated from our thoughts* also influences our damaged and exaggerated feeling reality. This process of generating feelings from the way we interpret the events around us automatically leads to trouble for codependents, because the experience of being abused damages our thinking. The process of assigning meaning to the events in our lives is skewed and the conclusions we draw are often inaccurate—but we don't know it. We believe our thinking is fine. But in fact our emotional responses to other people's actions toward us often seem bizarre to them.

In the process of generating feelings, we first bring some data into our inner world with one of our five senses. We hear a remark or we see a look on someone's face, for instance. To process this incoming data, we engage in thinking. We draw conclusions, and interpretations and give meaning to what we heard or saw (or tasted, smelled, or felt).

Out of this thinking comes our emotions about our thoughts. As a result of our emotions, we choose a behavior. If I interpret the remark I hear as a criticism, I may feel angry and make a sarcastic remark in return, or I may feel fear and withdraw from the relationship with the person who made the remark. If I interpret a look on someone's face as disapproval, I may feel shame and begin trying to please that person. In any case the remark brings pain or shame to me as a codependent, because of my interpretation of it as personal criticism. But let's say that I interpret the *same* remark as a compliment clothed as a playful joke from someone who loves me. *That* interpretation of the remark might lead to laughter and feelings of joy instead of pain—all because of my thinking.

CHART IV: How Thinking Can Affect Feelings and Behavior

Data →	Thinking →	Feelings →	Behavior
Remark	Criticism	Anger	Sarcastic response
Same Remark	Criticism	Fear	Withdrawal
Same Remark	Loving Friendliness	Joy	Laughter
Look on Face	Disapproval	Shame	People pleasing

We cannot change our emotions. What we feel is what we feel. In fact, it is dysfunctional to try *not* to be angry or *not* to be afraid when that is what we feel. To deal with an emotion we must acknowledge that we feel it and learn to express it appropriately. But we can examine the thinking we are doing that leads to the emotion.

Of course, I realize we can often choose a different behavior after we've had our feelings. For example, if I feel anger at your remark, I can choose to button my lip and not abuse you with my sarcasm. But I still have a large amount of anger bouncing around inside of me that I would not have to experience if I could think accurately and realize your remark was not criticism but a compliment. I believe that *examining the thinking* is far more effective in reducing the intensity of emotions we feel than changing our behavior. I strongly believe, however, that we must also try to express our emotions with healthy, nonabusive behaviors no matter what is triggering them.

What I seldom realize as a codependent is that because of my childhood abuse I tend to put a negative interpretation on incoming data when a positive interpretation might be far more accurate. My husband has very succinctly described the way my skewed thinking leads to irrational emotional flare-ups. (Actually, he says this isn't exactly what he said, but it is what I heard.) "Pia, you can take perfectly good data, and by the time it has gone through your mental process, it doesn't resemble reality at all. I don't know how you gave that kind of meaning to what I just said and did."

I "transform" incoming data as it goes through the grid of my abused past. I take the perception into my mind and give it meaning very different from what a functional person would give it. For example, when someone gives me a genuine compliment, because of my past abuse I can transform it into a subtle insult by labeling the remark as sarcasm. To make matters worse, I have no idea that I just did that; I think my brain is working perfectly well. I think it *was* sarcasm until the evidence is overwhelming that it was not.

Add to the fact that out of this feeling reality based on skewed thinking we then *act*, it's easy to see how we codependents are automatically set up for trouble and also don't understand why we're in trouble. We think we're acting quite normally. Consequently a relationship we have with a more functional person can be chaotic for that person as well as for us. On top of it all, we think *they* are acting strangely, being unreasonable or hypercritical.

WE CODEPENDENTS ARE SET UP TO ABUSE OUR CHILDREN AGAINST OUR WILL

The shame core, our load of carried feelings, and our skewed thinking all result in our experiencing much pain and confusion, isolation, and loneliness in our adult lives as codependents. Since it was our dysfunctional caregivers' shame core, load of carried feelings, and skewed thinking that prevented them from acting in our best interest and supporting us through our childhood developmental stages, it is clear that we, in turn, are almost guaranteed to be unable to parent our own children in a functional and supportive manner *until we face our own codependence* and move into recovery from it. As angry as we may be about what happened to us, as much as we desire to give our children the loving support we never had, we are virtually powerless to do so if we continue to deny our symptoms and how they impact others. The next chapter describes how we are likely to pass codependence on to our own children.

CHAPTER 7

From Generation to Generation

While the roots of codependence are in the childhood experiences of abuse, it is the shame core that perpetuates the disease from generation to generation. Whenever the shame core gives its message of being "less than" to a person, that person is automatically thinking, feeling, and behaving as a codependent.

A shame attack envelopes a parent and results in abuse to a child thus inducing the parent's shame into the child. That child grows up and has the same problems as the parent. So the shame-based parent creates a shame-based child who grows up and begets another child who is set up to be shame-based. And the process goes on and on. And to make matters more complex and serious, when a child has two shame-based parents, he or she gets a double load. I think that's why succeeding generations are getting more and more anxious and stressed as they experience compounded symptoms of codependence.

The following chart diagrams how the "roots" of the disease (child abuse) feed the "generator" of the disease (the shame core), which drives codependence (through the five core symptoms), and the adult's codependence results in planting the roots of the disease in his or her children (more child abuse).

CHART V: How the Shame Core Becomes the Generator That
Drives the Disease of Codependence

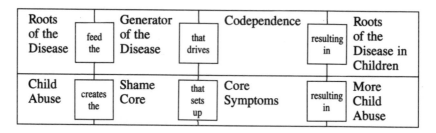

Roots of the Disease	feed the	Generator of the Disease	that drives	Codependence	resulting in	Roots of the Disease in Children
Child Abuse	creates the	Shame Core	that sets up	Core Symptoms	resulting in	More Child Abuse

Each symptom of codependence leads to specific forms of dysfunctional parenting.

- When we are unable to experience self-esteem from within
  but instead gather it from outside, we also are unable to
  appropriately esteem our children solely for who they are.
  Instead, we teach them other-esteem and praise them for their
  performance, their looks, their grades, and so on. We also are
  set up to shame them for their mistakes, their imperfections,
  and their other normal children's traits because we are basing
  our own esteem on them and their performance.

- When we do not have appropriate boundaries, we are very likely
  to disregard our children's vulnerability (since they have no
  boundaries) and abuse them. Also, we do not teach them how
  to develop boundaries – they imitate then introject our boundary system, which is not healthy. By our controlling we set ourselves up to be god or goddess of the family and interfere with
  the child's relationship to a power higher than we are. Or we
  set up someone else in the family (a spouse or a child) as our
  own Higher Power, also distorting the child's relationship to
  a Higher Power and ability to have spiritual experiences.

- When we cannot own and express our physical reality, our
  thoughts, our feelings, and our behavior, we in turn have little
  ability to allow our children to have their feelings, thoughts,
  behavior, and physical reality. While we are responsible for

guiding them to healthy ways of thinking, it is dysfunctional to tell them they "can't" or "shouldn't" feel what they feel or think what they think. It is dysfunctional to inordinately shame them or otherwise abuse them for the way they look, dress, or behave. Healthy parents confront what is not appropriate in a firm but supportive manner that respects the dignity of the child.

• When we have difficulty taking care of our adult needs and wants, we also have little ability to appropriately nurture our children. Too dependent parents often wind up teaching their children to meet the parents' needs instead of nurturing the children. Antidependent parents model for their children that it is shameful to ask for help. They often do not teach children how to meet their own needs adequately, especially the ones that require assistance from another person. And needless and wantless parents often wind up smothering the children, doing everything for them in a covert effort to meet their own needs and wants (of which they are unaware).

• When we have difficulty experiencing and expressing our own reality moderately, whether we are explosive or ice-cold, we have little ability to provide a stable environment for our children. Whether we are chaotic or supercontrolling, our children do not experience a stable home environment in which to mature. We also may not be aware of what to expect from children at each age level and therefore not respond when they need help to act their own age.

Chart VI on the following page summarizes these effects:

FAMILY SECRETS ARE REPEATED

Another way in which our codependence can affect our children is that any "secrets" or issues not dealt with from our own experiences of abuse often get acted out by the child. For example, if a mother was sexually abused at age fifteen, became pregnant, and

CHART VI: How the Core Symptoms Cause Less Than Nurturing Parenting

Core Symptoms of Codependence	Effect on Our Children
Difficulty experiencing appropriate levels of self-esteem	Inability to appropriately esteem our children
Difficulty setting functional boundaries	Inability to avoid transgressing our children's boundaries
Difficulty owning and expressing our own reality and imperfection	Inability to allow our children to have their reality and be imperfect
Difficulty taking care of our adult needs and wants	Inability to appropriately nurture our children and teach them to meet their needs and wants
Difficulty experiencing and expressing our reality moderately	Inability to provide a stable environment for our chidren

had an abortion, but never told anyone or dealt with the surrounding emotional trauma, her *daughter* may wind up getting pregnant and trying to sneak off to have an abortion, as if to signal the world that "there is a sexual abuse issue in this family." A young boy might become the neighborhood "peeping Tom," reflecting his father's undealt with childhood experience(s) with sexual abuse. This may sound bizarre to you but I see it often in my practice. Within this disease there are many sexual secrets.

I believe that this startling but common phenomenon is related to impaired boundaries. It isn't that the child can magically and consciously realize and act out the parent's secret. But since neither the child nor the parent has developed boundaries, the child sees or senses the sexually abused parent behaving inappropriately sexually in some covert way (because of the parent's undealt with abuse experience). The child repeats a similar behavior, having little or no idea originally that the behavior is inappropriate (the boy peeping in the neighbor's bedroom windows) or being driven by some inexplainable inner urge to ignore the family rules and do the sexual act anyway (a young girl having sex with her boyfriend or a "friendly" adult). Sometimes the child's experiencing a similar secret sexual encounter is not because of ignorance of appropriate behavior or a mysterious inner urge, but because the parent remains a victim. A small child may be molested by a baby-sitter that the parent, who had been abused by a baby-sitter, selected and trusted.

The family secret may be another issue, such as stealing, alcoholism, or vandalism, but it crops up again and again in the family history. And although reason rebels and says that we don't know for sure how this phenomenon takes place, only that it often *does*, I think undealt-with abuse and the lack of boundaries are deeply involved in the unconscious transmission of family secrets that get repeated for generations.

WHAT CONSTITUTES LESS-THAN-NURTURING EXPERIENCES?

Up to now we have spoken in general terms about dysfunctional parenting and less-than-nurturing or abusive experiences. Physical abuse, sexual abuse, emotional abuse, intellectual abuse, and spiritual abuse are all qualified to activate the shaming process that brings about adult codependence. Part Three contains a detailed description of each of these forms of abuse.

As a review, Chart VII on page 113 shows the complete development of codependence from the natural characteristics of a child, through the development of survival traits and core symptoms, to the way codependence affects the adults who have it and the children they raise.

CODEPENDENT SURVIVAL TRAITS CONDONED BY SOCIETY

It is important to note that the survival traits that develop in children are at either of two extremes and the adult symptoms of codependence are also at two extremes. Our society believes that people who exhibit the characteristics at one extreme—arrogance, invulnerability, perfectionism, antidependence, and "being in control"—are healthy, well-adjusted adults. However, the pain in their lives from unfulfilling relationships, unsatisfying careers, depression, and other problems would indicate that they are *not* functional adults. I believe that people exhibiting survival traits at either extreme are suffering from codependence.

CHART VII: Overview of Codependence

Natural Characteristics of a Child	Dysfunctional Survival Traits	Core Symptoms of Adult Codependence	Distorted Sense of Self and Dysfunctional Relationships†	Dysfunctional Parenting of Our Children
Valuable	Less-than or *Better-than	Difficulty experiencing appropriate levels of self-esteem	NEGATIVE CONTROL (controlling the reality of others for our own comfort)	Inability to appropriately esteem our children
Vulnerable	Too vulnerable or *Invulnerable	Difficulty setting functional boundaries	RESENTMENT (having a need to punish others for wrongs we perceive they have done to us)	Inability to avoid transgressing our children's boundaries
Imperfect	Bad/rebellious or *Good/perfect	Difficulty owning and expressing our own reality and imperfection	DISTORTED OR NONEXISTENT SPIRITUALITY (having difficulty experiencing connection to a power greater than self)	Inability to allow our children to have their reality and be imperfect
Dependent: needing, wanting	Too dependent or *Antidependent or Needless/wantless	Difficulty taking care of our adult needs and wants	AVOIDING REALITY (using addictions, physical illness or mental illness to avoid our own reality)	Inability to appropriately nurture our children
Immature	Extremely immature (Chaotic) or *Overmature (Controlling)	Difficulty experiencing and expressing our reality moderately	IMPAIRED INTIMACY (having difficulty sharing who I am with others and hearing them share who they are)	Inability to provide a stable environment for our children

* Our culture believes that the better-than, invulnerable, perfectionistic, antidependent, and controlling person is healthy. But in fact these are codependent characteristics and are much *more* difficult to treat than the characteristics at the other extreme: less-than, too vulnerable, rebellious, too dependent, and chaotic.
† The absence of horizontal lines in this column indicates that these elements are *not* related one-on-one with the other items across the same horizontal row, but result from any combination of the core symptoms and lead to any of the dysfunctional parenting components.

Part 3

THE ROOTS OF CODEPENDENCE

CHAPTER 8

Facing Abuse

Since codependence is the result of dysfunctional parenting that abuses the normal characteristics of children by harmful actions or by neglect, recovery involves reviewing your past to identify formative experiences in your early life that were less-than-nurturing or abusive. Getting your history straight is the second vital step in the process of recovery from codependence—facing its existence in your life was the first.

As you go over your early experiences, remember our broad definition of abuse—any experience that was less-than-nurturing or shaming. Just because certain behavior is considered culturally acceptable parenting does not mean it is actually nurturing to a child. If you *feel* a certain incident was inordinately shaming, even though "most parents" did it, it probably was indeed abusive.

SOME GUIDELINES TO HELP YOU EVALUATE YOUR OWN HISTORY

Here are some guidelines to assist in the process of getting your history straight.

1. Look at each year of your life from birth to age seventeen.
2. As you recall your history, identify what the shaming acts were and who did each to you. It is most often major care-

givers who were in a position of power or control over you and had access to you to abuse you—parents, surrogate parents, foster parents, or stepparents. Major caregivers can also be grandparents, foster grandparents, and step-grandparents. But children may also encounter abuse from older siblings, aunts, uncles, cousins, and other family members. It could be a minister, priest, nun, baby-sitter, Scout leader, teacher, Sunday school teacher, or coach. Some of the grossest incidents of sexual abuse men have brought to light in therapy were perpetrated by coaches in locker rooms. Children can also be abused by strangers.

3. It is very important NOT to focus on whether the person who did the abuse *meant* you harm or not. When you're at the point of getting your history straight, intention is irrelevant. My experience has been that the majority of the major caregivers who abused children did *not* mean to.

Trying to decide whether your major caregivers did or didn't intend to harm you can make you try to deny or minimize the abusiveness of what happened to you. It is likely that you won't write down any such "doubtful" incidents and talk about them. Abuse is abuse. Any abuse, intended or not, will have negative effects on a child. Adults are usually clearer about abuse they know was intended; unintended abuse is more difficult to bring to the surface and own as part of our history. So forget about intention when going over your past to identify abusive incidents.

4. Hold your abusers accountable but do not blame them. The purpose of acknowledging what really happened to you is to end the unconscious conspiracy to cover up the abusive behavior in your family. The goal of recognizing what really happened is to hold your major caregivers accountable in your mind, so that you can separate the abuse from the precious child who experienced it. Holding caregivers accountable does not mean that you accuse them of any-

thing. It just means owning your perception concerning what happened and getting in touch with the feeling reality that followed the less-than-nurturing events.

Having an accusatory mind-set leads you into a blaming process. *Blame* means you believe that you have the problems you have because of what somebody else did to you—and that's where it ends. It's as if you're saying, "I am who I am because of what you did to me, so I am helpless to change. It's all your fault. I'm going to focus only on what you did and I'm not going to move out of it." Blaming handcuffs you to the person who abused you and leaves you dependent upon that person's changing for you to have any recovery. This gives power to the offender and renders you, the victim, helpless—without the ability to protect yourself or change. Blaming will probably keep you stuck in the disease and is likely to make it even worse.

Accountability means that you acknowledge what happened and who did it, but that you can do what you need to do to protect yourself and make the changes necessary to recover from the abuse of your past. The process of accountability gives you the power to move into recovery and develop tools with which to deal with life, whether the offender ever changes or not.

5. Avoid comparing your history to someone else's. Such comparison can quickly lead you into minimization and denial. Wendy compares Janet's list to hers and says, "Janet was abused terribly. I'm not even going to say what happened to me. It doesn't compare at all." Whatever happened to you was important. If it seemed as though it was shaming to you, write it down. And remember that there is a *strong* tendency to minimize any shaming things your parents may have done.

6. Strike these four words from your vocabulary as you describe your history: "good," "bad," "right," and "wrong."

They're very judgmental words and using them in this context makes it hard to hold others accountable for what they did. We're afraid we are judging them as *being* "bad" people who *are* "wrong."

Instead, when describing behavior that was very painful, shaming, and failed to promote your best interests as a child, use the word "dysfunctional" rather than "wrong" or "bad." And when you talk about behavior that was helpful to you as a child, that was nurturing, that helped you feel good about yourself, use the word "functional" rather than "right" or "good."

7. Focus on *your* caregivers, *not on yourself as a caregiver.* Although you need to become accountable for your own dysfunctional parenting, moving your attention at this point to *your* behavior toward *your own* children can interfere with your recovery, because you're so busy focusing on "how horrible you are" that you can't see your encounters with abuse in your own childhood clearly. And *these* are the encounters that can lead to your recovery as a person and as a parent.

When you stay in the stance of "I am the cause of all these problems for my children," you are stuck in the disease, and continue to act out the blame your parents dumped on you during abuse. Caregivers often blame the child by saying, as they are abusing the child, "You caused me to beat (abuse) you. If you hadn't been late from school, I wouldn't have had to do this." As your parent (shamelessly) blamed you, the child, for his or her own abusive behavior, you probably believed you *were* responsible, and also felt your parent's shame as an overwhelming sense of inadequacy. Guilt about breaking a rule your parents held valuable would be in order, but the overwhelming shame comes from the fact that your parent used your fallibility as an opportunity to inordinately shame you. Then after you grew up and began trying to recover your history, you may feel that carried shame and turn away from what was done to you by your caregivers, looking instead at what kind of caregiver you have been, continuing to blame yourself as your caregivers blamed you.

A child is inordinately shamed when his or her sense of worth and value as a human being is discounted, and I believe that anything experienced as "inordinately shaming" is abuse whether the culture thinks it is abuse or not. Feelings of carried shame are hard for adults to face but are often what lead them to incidents in their history that turn out to be specific abusive experiences. And *acknowledgement of abuse* is vital for recovery from codependence.

8. As you review the five categories of abuse by major caregivers detailed in the following chapters (physical, sexual, emotional, intellectual, and spiritual), keep in mind the fact that abuse can also occur when children are shamed by their peers or society.

First, a child born with *an unusual physical feature or physical defect* often gets abused by other children for it. The feature might be big ears, big feet, buck teeth, being unusually tall and thin or unusually short or overweight, or having a physical handicap such as a large birthmark on the face, a deformed hand, or an illness that requires braces or a wheelchair. This kind of shame with regard to the body can interfere with the person's sexuality in adulthood.

Second, a child born into *a minority race*, whether black, Mexican-American, Chinese, or white—any race that is in the minority where the child grows up—may get attacked and shamed about his or her race.

A third thing that can make a child a target for peer abuse—and this is also something beyond the child's control—is when at an early age the child becomes aware that he or she has a different sexual orientation or preference and is *homosexual*. Some people have told me that at a very early age they knew that they were homosexual even though they didn't know the word for it. They felt extremely different from other people. When they finally did identify this "difference" and heard the general negative conversation in our culture about homosexuality, they were inadvertently shamed by "society."

REVIEWING OUR HISTORY IS A PREREQUISITE FOR RECOVERY

There are at least three reasons why looking at our past is vitally necessary to recovery and why failure to do so inhibits recovery. One is that as you bring up these childhood incidents and remember them, you can begin to see specifically how the parenting you received affected you. A second reason is that to recover, we must purge from our bodies the childhood feeling reality we had about being abused. The only way we can connect the feeling reality to what happened is to know what happened. And third, one of the well-documented characteristics of people who were raised in dysfunctional families is that as adults we often choose to relate to people who create the same emotional atmosphere we had in our family of origin. If we don't go back and look at how that happened, it is virtually impossible to look at the dysfunctional dynamics going on in our families today.

But most people cannot remember all of their history and some people have memory gaps spanning certain years in their childhood. What does it mean to have such memory gaps?

CHAPTER 9

Defenses Against Recognizing Abuse

Some patients come to treatment and realize that there are blank places in their memory about certain years in their childhood. They may not be able to remember anything before the age of six, for example, or they may not remember anything from between the ages of five and seven, but they can remember things before and after. As we shall see, part of the way children defend themselves from overwhelming experiences is to candy-coat the memories, so they are more pleasant, or put the memories out of conscious awareness using a myriad of protective devices called defense mechanisms.

DEFENSE MECHANISMS

Defense mechanisms are ways a healthy mind keeps from being overwhelmed by painful or threatening experiences. An example is the temporary numbness that blocks out feelings after the unexpected death of a close loved one. Under normal conditions the defense mechanism will withdraw in time, allowing the grieving person to experience his or her feelings accurately. But when the defense mechanisms work to *permanently* distort or hide feelings, it is difficult for a person to see and experience the reality of his or her life history.

We who were raised in dysfunctional families, in order to survive and grow to adulthood, had to use such defenses to block out abusive experiences that were too painful. The defenses may have worked very well when we were children and probably saved our sanity, our emotional stability, or our very lives as we were growing up. Without them we might have committed suicide, become mentally ill, or possibly not survived our childhoods in some other way. But as we grew up, these helpful and lifesaving defenses often moved beyond the necessary function of protection and turned into unyielding barricades that keep us from seeing the ego-threatening adult symptoms of the disease of codependence in ourselves.

Having a clear knowledge of what happens in our lives and being able to talk about it is a crucial part of facing codependence and moving on into recovery. Therefore, we need to know about these defense mechanisms and how they sabotage our clear knowledge of our lives today.

I will deal with six psychological defense mechanisms in this book. The first three, repression, suppression, and the more profound defense of dissociation, are first used primarily during childhood when we have overwhelming experiences. However, when these still operate in adulthood, they remove much of our history from our conscious minds. The defenses of minimization, denial, and delusion are those that apparently dirty the water most today when we adult codependents try to evaluate ourselves for codependence and go back over past memories to reconstruct our history.

CAUSES OF CONFUSING OR DISTRESSING BEHAVIOR

When our defense mechanisms block out memories of our abusive family of origin, we may grow up and marry someone *just like* the opposite-sex parent who abused us—without being able to see that this is true. If we have distorted or blocked some or all of our memories of growing up, we are blind to any resemblance between a prospective spouse and the abusive parent. Because of defense mechanisms we aren't aware that we have married someone who can help us reproduce all or parts of the familiar abusive system in which we were raised. Also, since we can't see the reality of our own thinking, feeling, and behaving as adults in an abusive relationship when our defense mechanisms are at work, we cannot really understand and act on the fact that it is possible for us to develop different responses to seemingly "no win" situations. Instead we believe we're crazy, the primary complaint that most codependents offer when they first come for help. "I feel nuts. Something's disconnected." Defense mechanisms disconnect us from the reality of our lives.

Not having access to our history or having a distorted version of it contributes to the sense of craziness. Having a clear picture of our history can be the doorway to freedom from these crazy feelings and from being controlled by our past. Learning about these defense mechanisms can help us begin to recognize them and how they may be blocking us from seeing not only our history but our current symptoms and unmanageability.

REPRESSION, SUPPRESSION, AND DISSOCIATION

Repression, suppression, and dissociation are used by children to cope with traumatic experiences of abuse. These mechanisms remove from conscious memory an experience that otherwise would overwhelm a child. Such traumatic experiences would otherwise keep abused children in so much pain and fear they couldn't stand it. If you have such blank places in your history, you may have needed to use one of these three processes to protect yourself.

Repression is the automatic and unconscious forgetting of things that are too painful to remember. *Suppression* is consciously choosing to forget things that are too painful to remember. *Dissociation* involves a child's psychologically separating "who he or she is" from his or her body during the abusive act and taking that inner "self" away somewhere where the abuse cannot be seen, heard, felt, or experienced in any way. Children usually reserve dissociation to survive abuse they feel is life-threatening. The fear is that either "who they are" is going to be destroyed, or that they'll be physically destroyed in situations such as incest, molestation, or being severely beaten.

In repression painful and frightening memories are automatically shifted into the unconscious mind where they are for all intents and purposes lost. As an adult the person who has repressed an incident cannot get to this material by a conscious act of will; it's simply not available. On the other hand, suppressed material can often be recalled, since the act of suppression is more the result of conscious intention.

For example, as a child, Brad watched his father beat up his mother. He saw her lying on the floor with blood on her face. If he used repression he wouldn't be able to remember later that the beating happened. On the other hand, if he were to suppress the same scene, he'd have said to himself consciously as he watched, "This scene is too terrible to remember and I'm going to forget it." And he would. Whether Brad used repression or suppression, he remained cognitively aware *during* the abuse and experienced all of it: he saw it, he felt his feelings about it, and had some thoughts about it.

In both cases the information about the scene goes into the unconscious mind, but if Brad used repression, the disappearance happened without his awareness and the repressed material is *not available to him* to recall even if he (in childhood or later as an adult) wants to. Suppressed material, however, can often be remembered with conscious effort, or when reading about abuse, realizing that adult symptoms indicate that something abusive happened in childhood, and thinking hard about it.

When Brad, as an "adult child," comes to therapy, he presents himself in a way that shows he is still using these defenses of repression and suppression. The clue I pick up is that when I ask him to tell me about his childhood, he doesn't have any childhood history or it is very fragmented. He doesn't remember certain years, certain periods, things about a certain person, or he says something like, "I don't remember anything, Pia. How can I tell you my history if I don't have a history?"

But as I talk about the different kinds of abuse, Brad may suddenly experience the return of a suppressed memory and say, "Well, my gosh, that same thing happened to me! I'd totally forgotten it!" So with some outside help, such as listening to a lecture, reading a book about child abuse, or being in group with someone who had experiences like his, Brad's unconscious mind can begin to release his own suppressed history to him.

Dissociation removes an event as completely from the child's conscious mind as repression does and occurs when the child's body stays in the room and continues to receive the abuse, but emotionally and mentally the child "goes away." Although the physical pain is felt, and the body of the child is still being abused, emotionally and mentally, the child is absent and doesn't "feel" the abuse after dissociation. With repression and suppression, however, the child continues to experience the full force of the abuse as it is happening in all three areas: physically, mentally, and emotionally.

During a dissociative experience, the child's conscious mind usually goes to one of at least three "places" (there may be more). Each place is successively more guarded and harder to get to later than the previous one. The first place is to move horizontally, and be lying, sitting, or standing next to one's body, observing what's happening a little bit but not feeling anything. The second place is to move vertically, floating up above what's happening (or down below), sometimes looking down on it (or up at it), but not feeling what is happening. The third place is to disappear down inside the self, not seeing, feeling, or hearing anything. The sensation is often described as being inside a black hole. If the child has gone in this third place, the memory of what happened is very hard to retrieve later in therapy. This third place, I believe, is reserved for the most extreme forms of abuse.

As an adult who comes for therapy, the person with a dissociative experience presents himself or herself much like a person who has used repression. There are memory gaps in his or her history. But the memory of an abusive experience during which a child dissociated can be retrieved by the adult child in the form of a spontaneous regression.

It would be very unusual for a spontaneous regression to happen to you while reading about any issues of abuse in this book, but I will describe it here so you will know what one is. A spontaneous regression is a process by which memories lost through dissociation can be retrieved. It almost always happens in a therapeutic situation, guided by a counselor. It may happen spontaneously in a group therapy setting when the content of the group's work triggers a dissociated memory in someone, as the term "spontaneous" implies. But more often it is an experience that a counselor guides a person into using therapeutic techniques.

During a spontaneous regression, people are somehow transported back in their history into dramatically reexperiencing a traumatic childhood event. In the normal conversation of therapy retrieval of repressed or suppressed memories may take place as a more detached mental experience, but people experiencing a spontaneous regression, sitting with eyes closed, have the sense of *reliving* the event, including the same intense feelings they had when the event was taking place, and their bodies are often contorted in almost the same movements they made when they were children trying to escape the pain. Because the unconscious mind has no sense of chronological time, when the memory of this abuse returns, the patient is transported in his or her mind back to the time it happened. In this way the healing of the pain of that past event can take place in the context in which it occurred. The patient reexperiences the abusive event *as if he or she were at the same age* when it happened. Afterward, the abused child returns to his or her adult age in the therapy room.

Sometimes individuals dissociate again during the regression, but the difference between the original dissociation and the one during a therapeutic regression is that in the latter they are being supported and helped by the therapist and will be able to remember what happened during the spontaneous regression after it is over, even if some of the facts of the abuse event are lost to them.

Of course, since patients were perceiving the abuse through their child-aged senses, (sight, hearing, smell, and so on) the specific details may have gotten confused or distorted. But the important issue for therapy is that some kind of abuse did take place that gave them as children an extra burden of induced feelings still crippling them as adults.

Attempting to retrieve dissociative memories with your sponsor or other untrained friend is dangerous and should be avoided. Although a therapeutically induced regression is a frightening experience, it is also a wonderful process in therapy for retrieving taboo memories loaded with crippling fear, pain, anger, and shame.

MINIMIZATION, DENIAL, AND DELUSION

Often in therapy we encounter ego-threatening material or material that might threaten the continuation of an addiction, this material just "disappears" and we cannot remember it, even during a specific confrontation. The defenses of minimization, denial, and delusion can also cause us to skew our opinion of our present behavior as well as our history.

Minimization means I reduce the significance of what I do, think, or feel and make it seem *less* serious or important than if someone else did, thought, or felt the same thing. For example, I tell myself that my being overwhelmed with responsibilities, always tired and irritable because I have become overcommitted isn't really so bad. I tell myself that as soon as I get organized I can handle it. But when I hear my friend Wanda complain about the same thing, having no time for herself and being exhausted and cross with *her* children, co-workers, husband, and friends because *she* has overcommitted *herself*, I think, "Well, can't she *see* that she's overcommitted? Why doesn't she let go of some of her responsibilities? She's headed for a nervous breakdown!" I recognize my own state of overcommitment, but I talk myself out of accepting the level of havoc it wreaks and how unmanageable my life has actually become. I "minimize" it.

In childhood, minimization works like this. Terry watches her father beat up her mother. She is shocked and horrified, but she minimizes the event by saying to herself when it happens, "Well, this happened, and I really hurt, but it's not as bad as all that." The memory of the event remains in her conscious mind. Terry can talk about it, and describe it, and she knows it happened. But as a child, she talks herself out of experiencing the full impact of her feelings, even though she vaguely knows "something's wrong" with her feelings about the beating.

Later, when Terry as an adult comes to therapy and hears my lecture about child abuse, she is still likely to use minimization and discount the seriousness of the effect of seeing her father beat up her mother. I pick this up when she says to me, "I hear it's abusive for a child to watch Dad beat up Mom, and I know it happened to me, yet in *my case* it wasn't that bad."

Another common example of minimization is when someone accuses an alcoholic of being drunk. The accused person may claim and actually believe that the amount of liquor consumed was only "a couple of drinks" (when in fact he or she drank a quart of Scotch). That person is using minimization.

But with *denial*, I tell myself there is *nothing wrong at all* with my state of overcommitment, although it may be too much for someone else. Life is just this way and I must make the best of it. My schedule isn't too full—everyone has a lot to do. I have complete awareness of how much I must accomplish each day, but I'm unaware of the sense of being overwhelmed and the anger, fear, and pain that accompanies the immense workload. I deny my own bizarre, overcommitted state. And yet I can clearly see that *Wanda's* life is out of control because of her overcommitment.

In childhood, Terry's denial works like this. She watches the beating of her mother by her father, experiences the abuse, and says to herself, "There's really *nothing wrong* with this argument between my parents." She has cognitive awareness of the beating but experiences no feelings because she "denies" the seriousness of the event.

And when she becomes an adult, her use of denial as a defense against the pain of that abuse continues to operate. She listens to me talk about child abuse. I might give an example in my lecture about a girl I call Cindy who as a child watched her father beat her mother. When Terry hears me say to her that it's very abusive for a child to be allowed to watch a parent beat up another parent, she would say something like, "Pia, I agree that watching the beating was abusive for Cindy, but it wasn't abusive *at all in my case*."

If an alcoholic in *denial* in accused of being drunk, he or she may claim that while drinking a quart of Scotch might make some-one else drunk, it's not enough Scotch to make him or her drunk. "I hold my liquor better than that, and I am *not* drunk!" Denial operates when we can see and grasp certain realities in *other peoples' lives*, but can't see the same realities in our own lives.

The process of *delusion* is more profound and serious. Delusion means we believe something in spite of clear facts to the contrary, which means we can hear the facts, but we don't assign the proper meaning to them. For example, I have a friend who was blatantly sexually abused by his mother when he was a child. But he refused to believe that what she did was sexually abusive because she just "wasn't that kind of woman." His delusion about his mother's character was stronger for him than the *facts* of her *actually* sexually abusing him.

In adulthood, when I am in delusion, I believe that my chronic state of overcommitment and the constant high-speed schedule I keep up with is normal and healthy. When I hear someone talk about how unhealthy it is to keep ourselves under so much stress and hear them say that we need to have quiet time, leisure time, fun time, I say to myself—that just *isn't true*. A real person leading a real life just can't do all that. It might be nice, but it isn't realistic. And in my delusion I may tell my friend Wanda the same thing: "Shape up, girl! Having all these things to do is just the way life is. There's nothing wrong. Maybe you're tired and irritable because you're coming down with the flu. You just need a better attitude." My delusion that my constant working is normal and healthy is so strong, it even spills over to include others.

As a therapist, I would know that delusion was in operation for Terry if she heard my lecture about Cindy watching her father beat her mother and said to me, "Pia, I hear you tell me that what Cindy saw is abusive to her, but it just isn't. The parents were just having a normal fight. Nobody was hurting Cindy. If two people want to fight that way, it's okay with me." Her delusion is that it is not harmful to a child for parents to physically attack each other in front of that child.

But the facts are that a child *is* abused by watching one of the two most important and necessary caregivers in his or her life beat another one up. A person in delusion can "hear the facts" but can't accept them as being true, so he or she acts as if the awful reality isn't awful.

Delusion runs rampant in codependence, so recognizing it in ourselves is important. We experience the symptoms of codependence in our adult lives leading to painful emotional consequences for ourselves and those we love, yet our delusion is that, with enough time, "things will just work out." And although we have often seen things in our lives and relationships that are very painful or scary, we codependents in delusion live as if these things were *not* painful or scary. And we sometimes stay in very abusive situations and relationships without facing the reality that we are being seriously abused.

Like all the other defense mechanisms, delusion is invisible to us, making it a serious problem: we don't know we are deluded. We live in an unreal world based on our delusions, but *we see that unreal world as reality.* Because we can't afford to hear the facts about our lives as they really are, we often get very angry with people who try to point out any fallacies in our delusions. This position leaves us very vulnerable, since both reality itself and anyone with a strong sense of reality tend to threaten the view we have of our world. People in delusion tend to isolate themselves from those who might reveal the truth about their lives.

Often the resistance to my confrontation of delusion in people in therapy stems from the fact that these persons are *repeating* the same dysfunctional behavior they received as children with their own children and don't want to recognize it as dysfunctional. People in this situation can't see their own resistance to a change of perception. They just stick to the distorted "facts" of their own deluded view.

Critical to recovery from codependence is knowing both what defense mechanisms are and how they work in our lives. Accepting the following facts can aid recovery greatly:

- Defense mechanisms still operate in adult codependents.
- Our own defenses are usually invisible to us.
- To recover, we must allow other trusted people to confront those defenses by telling us when they think we are using them.
- Although it will be hard and we may feel fear or anger at the time, we must listen to these confrontations to break through the defenses into recovery.

You may encounter some of these resistances to facing your own reality as you read about the symptoms of codependence and the descriptions of abuse in this book.

BODY MEMORIES AND FEELING MEMORIES

Two helpful indicators that, if followed, often lead to a recovery of lost history are body memories and feeling memories. These are like security passwords to a carefully guarded computer program. Once the computer operator enters the password into the computer, the operator has access to the program. In a similar way, once a person recognizes a frightening or painful feeling or body memory, he or she may be able to follow that memory and gain access to data in the unconscious mind about frightening or painful abuse that was repressed or dissociated from when it originally happened. This valuable data can then be brought to the conscious mind of the patient (with the help of a skillful therapist), so that the person can work through the feelings around the memory and begin to heal from it.

A *body memory* is a sudden physical symptom that doesn't appear to be related to any physical cause at the moment. For example, you may be sitting comfortably, reading this book, but all of a sudden you get a piercing pain in your head, you feel dizzy, or you feel a wave of nausea. It may be that suddenly your arm feels like it's been kicked or that someone has put a hand on your throat and is choking you. Or suddenly you feel like there's a hand on the back of your neck and it's pinching you. Or you may feel a pain in the area of your groin. Such sensations are body memories.

A *feeling memory* is a sudden overwhelming emotional experience that also cannot be explained by anything that you are aware of at the moment. Feeling memories surface mostly in the form of four primary emotions: anger, fear, pain, and shame. I also call feeling memories "feeling attacks" since they seem to come suddenly and uninvited out of nowhere. I call a feeling attack in the form of anger a "rage attack," and one in the form of fear a "panic attack" or "paranoia attack." A feeling memory of pain is a sudden overwhelming sense of hopelessness often followed by a thought of suicide or believing one will die from the intense pain. A "shame attack" is a sudden, profound, almost overwhelming sense of being "less than," worth less, inadequate, bad, stupid, or ugly (derogatory words about ourselves often come to us in the process of a shame attack).

Body and feeling memories indicate to me that although our minds are powerful enough to bury memories in our unconscious mind and "know but not know," the body never forgets the painful experience of abuse and will keep trying to let us see the truth about ourselves.

For example, when I give a lecture about this subject, often someone in the audience says, "Pia, I'm having one of those memories. It feels like there is a hand on the back of my neck and I'm so scared." The hand on the neck experience is a body memory and the fear about the hand is a feeling memory.

A feeling memory is always experienced as an overwhelming feeling. Let's say a woman in a therapy group who is hearing my lecture suddenly has a feeling memory of fear. She goes into a condition that is close to panic and says something like, "I don't know what's going on, Pia, but I'm so scared I want to run out of this room!"

Then I ask her, "Would you tell me what was going on when you started to feel the panic? What was I talking about?"

And she might say, "When you started talking about a little girl being sexually penetrated by her father, I went into such a panic that I practically left."

Then I ask, "Is it possible that someone sexually abused you?" because such a question at that point could very well trigger the return of a lost memory.

Many times these feeling and body memories can be used as doorways to take yourself back into remembering what really did happen in your childhood and retrieving long repressed events. So in a few pages, when you start to read about the different kinds of abuse, start paying attention to any body and feeling memories you may have.

FACING YOUR DEFENSES

If you are a codependent, you may have found it necessary during childhood to protect yourself with one of the six defense mechanisms I have described. Minimization, denial, delusion, repression, suppression, and dissociation are almost always operating in codependents, for they allowed you to survive encounters that would have driven you mad or overwhelmed you in some other way. Therefore, as you read the following descriptions of abuse, be aware that they are very likely still operating in you and allow for them as you proceed.

Our society supports parenting techniques that we now know are less than nurturing for the child. Children in dysfunctional families may appear to be well-behaved, well-adjusted, high-achieving, successful members of the family, or they may seem to be spoiled, tyrannical, chaotic, disruptive members. As we've seen, either set of characteristics may reflect the internal adaptations such children have made to survive in these dysfunctional families. We now know that these adjustments lead to codependence in adulthood. The following pages include descriptions of less-than-nurturing, or abusive, practices of children's caregivers.

CHAPTER 10

Physical Abuse

All forms of abuse (physical, sexual, emotional, intellectual, or spiritual) can be either overt or covert. And abuse can be either empowering or disempowering to the victim.

OVERT VERSUS COVERT ABUSE

Overt abuse is out in the open. Everybody can see it; the child really knows about it because the reality of it is so clear. *Covert abuse* is hidden, devious, and indirect. It is comprised of things that are suggested rather than visible. It encompasses manipulation rather than straightforward control of a child. Covert abuse also includes certain kinds of parental neglect, such as neglect of the emotional nurturing or physical nurturing needs of a child. The effects of covert abuse are more difficult to recover from because they are so hard for people to identify. People have a hard time claiming the damage to themselves resulting from "under the rug" experiences since they never "saw the abuse go by." An example of covert abuse might be a mother who withdraws love and approval (emotionally abandons her children) unless they submit to her control.

EMPOWERING VERSUS DISEMPOWERING ABUSE

Abuse either empowers or disempowers. When abuse disempowers, it shames children, robs them of their value, and makes them "less-than" people.

Empowering abuse teaches children incorrectly that they are better than others. Since all of us have equal value, teaching people that they are superior to others is erroneous and dysfunctional.

The result of empowering experiences is that children grow up to become offenders or victimizers. If a child experiences disempowering abuse along with the empowering abuse, then the child may bounce back and forth between "I am less than" versus "I am better than"; the amount of time spent in one position compared with the other is based on the amount of either type of abuse. People with a mixture of both empowering and disempowering abuse are very treatable.

The children who *get empowered, and never disempowered*, are often in a difficult position in that they are "self will run riot," controlling people by abusive behavior that gets out of control. They often are very offensive and may believe they are entitled to take from others and use others.

PHYSICAL ABUSE

The way the major caregivers treat a child's body determines whether physical abuse has occurred or not. Was the child's physical person treated with respect, or was it attacked or ignored? Whenever a caregiver attacks a child's body in some way, by beating the child with an object, slapping, pinching, pulling the hair or banging the head, physical abuse takes place. The child experiences painful touching, loses his or her self-respect, and absorbs the caregiver's shame.

If a father physically abuses his son, for instance, the son's experience of the attack on his body tells him that his body is not worth being respected (that his body is an object of shame) and that he has no right to be free from painful touches; and he has no right to control what happens to his body. In effect, the father takes control of his son's body and says, "I can do whatever I want with this body."

ABUSE DISGUISED AS DISCIPLINE

Many times physical abuse occurs under the guise of good discipline. I consider functional physical discipline of a child within the family to be nothing more than a flat hand applied to a covered bottom done in such a way that the child is not bruised, there are no red marks, his or her little brains don't get shaken, and the parent doesn't induce inordinate shame into the child as a result. Using a flat hand makes it possible for the parent to feel when he or she is hurting the child too much, because the parent's hand will hurt. A covered bottom means the child is not stripped, exposed, or shamed sexually by having his or her pants pulled down. Also, I think that when children are very young, it is appropriate discipline to lightly spank their hands when they're putting them into things you don't want them to be in.

This functional physical discipline is more of an attention-getting device by the parent than administration of punishment. The child's own natural shame will be triggered when the parent points out his or her imperfection, but functional discipline includes assuring the child that it is the behavior that needs confronting; the child is a precious, wonderful person who just needs to notice his or her imperfection and deal with it when it leads to harmful or antisocial behaviors.

Sometime around age six it is not, in my opinion, even appropriate to use a hand on the covered bottom. Instead, the parent can explain what is unacceptable about what the child is doing, point out how the child needs to change, and say what the consequences will be if he or she does not change. The parent also follows through and delivers these unpleasant consequences to the child, if he or she does not follow the parent's guidance. For example, if a teenage son comes in late, you don't beat him; you respond with something like, "Tomorrow night you're not to go out."

It's important to understand the difference between "behavior and consequences" and "crime and punishment." The consequences should be, if possible, a reasonable follow-up related to what has happened and of like "weight" in the child's mind to the offending behavior. For example, a teenager might be grounded for one night for coming in late once, but not grounded for two weeks.

The following is a helpful example from Virginia Satir's book *Peoplemaking*, in which she describes the difference between consequences and punishment. Let's say your son in junior high starts to forget his lunch every day. He calls you, his mother, and you take him his lunch. To stop this behavior pattern, you sit down with him and say, "Look, Charlie, the normal consequences of not making arrangements for lunch is that you go hungry." Then when he forgets his lunch the next day and calls you again, you say, "I'm sorry. We talked about this last night. The normal consequence of your not taking lunch with you is for you to be hungry. I'm not bringing your lunch."

The consequence should be as close as possible to what would happen if there were no family member there to intervene in the behavior of a child. In other words, if a person were disruptive in a public place, he might be arrested and sent to jail. If someone were disruptive at a movie, the usher might have to throw her out of the movie theater. So if a young boy is disruptive at home in the den while everyone is trying to watch television, it would be appropriate to remove him from the room and put him where he will not disturb others, perhaps in his own room. It is explained to him that his disruptive behavior is not acceptable to the family and that he needs to be away from the family until he can stop disrupting.

Functional parenting does not include physically attacking a child. While I certainly do not advocate anarchy in the family, I do strongly assert that the functional approach to the child is one of care. It's as if that child's body is like a $25,000 vase. It isn't safe to slap it, kick it, punch it, and toss it about because it's so valuable and might get damaged. A parent can break a child's spirit and sense of worth with this kind of abuse just as that valuable vase would break with careless or intentional abusive handling.

ABJECT PHYSICAL ABUSE

Abject abuse, which most people recognize is wrong and illegal, includes such extreme forms of physical abuse as burning or scalding a child on purpose, cutting off a child's hands, burning a child's genitals with a lighted cigarette, fracturing a child's skull, or giving a child lacerated internal organs from punishing blows. While it is clear that in such cases the parent's attitude toward the child's body is not one of respect, there are other forms of physical abuse that can have harmful consequences for the child because of the shaming process that accompanies the behaviors.

USE OF IMPLEMENTS

Some people strike their children with an implement such as a belt, or hairbrush, a chair, a spatula, a piano leg, a switch from a bush out in the yard, a shoe, a wooden spoon, or a fly swatter. Whenever such things are used to punish a child, it is very probable that abuse is taking place. Attacking a child with an implement is very shaming and the parent has no idea how much pain is being inflicted, because he or she can't feel it.

As a child gets older, physical discipline works less and less well anyway. I had someone complain to me saying, "Well, my ten-year-old will not respond to discipline. I have to beat him really hard to get him to respond." Children become more and more able to endure and resist. When they get to be about thirteen or fourteen, if they're as big as the parent, they may well start attacking the parent, because that's what the parent has been teaching them to do through severe physical punishment.

OTHER FORMS OF PHYSICAL ATTACK

Face slapping, although one of the more common kinds of physical abuse, is particularly shaming. I believe it is possibly one of the worst kinds of nonabject physical abuse because the face is such a visible and recognizable symbol of a person's identity.

Hair pulling, head banging, ear pulling, pinching, or shaking a child are also abusive, because the child's body is not being treated with respect or even safety. A child's brain is very delicate. A cerebral contusion can occur when you take a precious little head and bang it against the wall or take two precious little heads and bang them together.

One of the ways we can conceive of why these things are abusive is to imagine an adult striking or pulling the hair of another adult. It is unacceptable for me to walk up and yank your hair, take your head and bash it against the wall, pull your ears, slap your face, or shake you—regardless of what you may have said to me. It's a very disrepectful act against your body. In our culture we can see that for an adult to treat another adult that way is wrong, and we oppose such acts with legal measures. For instance, if I did any of those things to you, you could have me arrested. The same idea of respect should hold true for a child.

SEXUAL-PHYSICAL ABUSE

Some people use physical abuse of their children—"discipline" —as a way to sexually stimulate themselves. Some physical beatings are sexual-physical beatings and are a form of sexual-physical abuse, because the parent is stimulating himself or herself sexually by contact with the child. It's usually a ritualized beating and to the child there seems to be something mysterious and frightening about it. It's very systematic, structured, repetitive, open, aggressive, and unpredictable as to when it will happen (from the child's point of view).

TICKLING A CHILD INTO HYSTERIA

Some kinds of tickling are physically abusive. I don't mean that "coochy-coochy-coo" under the chin kind that almost everybody does with babies. I mean the kind of tickling where the father, for instance, holds his daughter down and tickles her into hysteria, so that she is either laughing or crying hysterically and feeling totally out of control of her own body. She sometimes wets her pants. This abuse can be done to boys as well as girls, of course, and can be done by any family member, including older siblings or aunts and uncles. The person doing the tickling is in effect taking hold of the child's body and treating it like an object. The message is "I'm the parent. I can do whatever I want with your body, since I'm god or goddess of the family. I'm going to put you down on the floor and tickle you into hysteria and I have the right to do that." It's inappropriate and can be a painful and shaming experience for the child.

Sometimes such tickling may be a covert form of sexual-physical abuse. The tickling may shift from physical abuse, in which an adult is just discharging a lot of displaced anger, into sexual abuse when the parent is sexually stimulating himself or herself by the tickling.

LACK OF OR TOO MUCH PHYSICAL NURTURING

Appropriate physical nurturing is one of the basic dependency needs of a child and is most needed by an infant. As children age, they should be allowed to take more control over who touches them and when touching happens to their bodies. If physical nurturing at the beginning doesn't take place or if it doesn't diminish later, the results are abusive.

Physical nurturing of infants includes hugging, holding, touching, rocking, walking close to, and being close. This gives children the impression that they are touchable, that their little bodies are precious, and that you know how to soothe them physically. This sort of physical nurturing is so important, that if little babies under the age of a year old don't get enough of it, they may die.

Lack of appropriate physical nurturing is an experience of physical abuse. When a child does not get enough physical nurturing, the message to the child from the caregiver is, "I don't want to touch you. Don't touch me. Everybody's cold and nobody's supposed to touch."

A person who had too little physical contact in childhood has the same problem in adulthood as the person who was slapped, kicked, or hit. In the attack, the child learns that touch is physically painful. But the child who doesn't get touched also finds it painful to be touched—*emotionally* painful. And since it's unfamiliar and frightening to have physical contact with anyone, he or she shies away from it. The reasons for not wishing to be touched are different (emotional pain versus physical pain), but the behavioral effect is very similar.

At the other extreme, too much touching, too much holding, too much physical enmeshment—especially in the later years—smothers the child.

The child may grow up demanding more physical touching and hugging than is comfortable for his or her spouse or family members to give to feel loved and secure.

THE GRADUAL DIMINISHING OF PHYSICAL NURTURING

Initially children need a lot of physical nurturing, but as they develop, they become more autonomous and the amount of physical nurturing needed diminishes. If the parent doesn't reduce that intense physical nurturing over time, the physical enmeshing overwhelms the child. A child who experiences overwhelming physical nurturing often thinks, "Oh, my gosh. Here comes Mom. She's going to KISS me! Let me get away from her. She's just too much."

For example, when little Ginny is an infant, she needs a lot of very direct physical nurturing. She needs to be held, hugged, patted, and rocked a lot while she is awake. But as Ginny ages, she will naturally not want all that closeness. She becomes curious about the rest of the world. Her mother can pick her up and hug her and she thinks, "That's fine," and then she wants to get out of her mother's lap and go play.

But by the time Ginny starts walking, her mother, if functional, starts backing off somewhat, gradually diminishing physical contact and letting Ginny come to her rather than going to Ginny so much. When she is a little older and learns to talk, Ginny learns to come to her mother and say, in essence, "I'm hurting. Will you hug me?" And so the mother shifts from always directly initiating physical contact with her daughter to gradually diminishing it, letting Ginny tell her when she wants nurturing and when she has had enough.

But at the same time, the parents' vigilance doesn't stop until the child is approximately between age ten and twelve. Up to that point parents still need to watch closely for signals of the child's need for physical nurturing. The child may be hurting and needing the parent but may not know how to ask. So parents should approach and say something like, "Tell me what's going on. Is it okay if I touch you? Do you need a hug?" Initially parents hug and touch a lot without asking. The older the child gets, the more parents let the child determine the intensity of the nurturing. And then when the child gets up somewhere between ten and twelve years of age, he or she will usually shift to the attitude, "I want to tell you when I want a hug. Don't touch me without my permission."

I still approach my eleven-year-old and physically nurture him without a whole lot of permission and without him asking for it although I am beginning to back off. But I might walk up and put my hand on his shoulder. I've got a sixteen-year-old whom I wouldn't think of touching without some sort of negotiation such as, "Do you want a hug?" Most of the time I let him come to me, but I watch and am aware of him. Sometimes I ask him if he wants to come and get a hug, but I don't automatically walk up and touch him. I let my twenty-year-old negotiate all physical contact between us. I might watch and may say something to him, but it's now his responsibility to ask for physical nurturing.

Of course there are individual differences in the needs different children experience for closeness, but I have tried to indicate a general approach to this aspect of physically nurturing children. In families where the earlier physical nurturing has been lacking or unhealthy, codependents may find it necessary to discuss any *changes* they have learned they should make in their behavior with the family, so the members won't experience the change as abuse (e.g., unless a mother explains why she had decided to suddenly back off from her usual constant showering of attention on a son, he may wonder "what he did wrong" or why his mom "doesn't love him anymore").

WATCHING PHYSICAL ABUSE DONE TO SOMEONE ELSE

Watching another person being abused is profoundly abusive. A daughter might have been a "perfect little adult" in behavior, but her brother might have been beaten on a routine basis because he rebelled. And the daughter might have had to sit and listen to the thumping and screaming while the brother was abused or actually had to watch it, because Dad would line everybody up and make the kids watch each other get beaten. That child who had to watch often feels the full effect of the abuse in terms of emotional pain. The message to the child watching is, "This can happen to you. Shape up." And it can generate a great deal of fear.

One of the most difficult cases I ever had to work with con-cerned a woman whose mother had emotionally opted out of the family, ignored everything that was going on, and left an eighteen-month-old baby in my client's care when she was only six years old. Also, beginning at age six, she was a victim of repeated vaginal intercourse by her father. During the same period of time the father was physically attacking her eighteen-month-old brother.

When the six-year-old girl was being sexually attacked herself, she would dissociate, going somewhere else in her mind so she couldn't feel what was happening to her. But when her brother was being abused, she could not do that, because she was the major caregiver for him. So she watched and waited for her father to drop the baby, so she could pick him up and take care of him.

When we did her debriefing and shame reduction work, I was surprised to realize that her own experience of incest was a lot easier to work on than her experience of watching the brother being attacked.

NEGLECT AND ABANDONMENT OF PHYSICAL DEPENDENCY NEEDS

Neglect and abandonment occur more often with regard to the need for physical nurturing (as we've just seen) and emotional nurturing (discussed in chapter 12). But physical abuse also occurs when a child's physical dependency needs aren't met, such as the need for nourishing food, adequate clothing, safe, clean shelter, and medical and dental attention.

Neglect means that the parent tried to meet these needs but didn't know how or didn't meet them well enough to avoid shaming the child. Perhaps there was food on the table but it wasn't enough, or it wasn't well balanced and nutritious, so the child wound up hungry a lot, or underweight and scrawny, or obese, or having lots of dental problems. Perhaps the house or apartment was too crowded to provide adequate privacy, or was in a dangerous neighborhood, or in need of repair. Perhaps the wallpaper was badly stained and peeling at the corners, or the bathroom door didn't close properly and never got repaired. Perhaps the children did not get taught how to properly brush their teeth and wound up having to endure painful dental work as a result. Perhaps they didn't get taken to the emergency room when they accidentally got cut, so the wound healed with an ugly scar, or it became infected and they wound up being hospitalized and in danger of losing an arm or leg.

Abandonment means that little or no attempt was made to meet the child's physical needs. Perhaps neither parent cooked at all and the children learned to survive by ordering pizza delivered or eating junk food they prepared themselves, or they starved except for food they got at school. Perhaps the parents did not provide a place to live and the family drifted, living with relatives until asked to leave. A friend of mine experienced abandonment of her need for dental care. She was never taught how to care for her teeth nor taken to a dentist. All her teeth had to be removed when she was in her twenties and she began wearing dentures.

As we've seen, whether children's caregivers attack them with painful touching or ignore their need for physical contact, the results are experiences that cause inordinate shame in children, hindering their growth into mature adults.

CHAPTER 11

Sexual Abuse

Although a child has a natural capacity to respond to sexual stimulation in a childlike way, whenever an adult is being sexual with a child, the experience is abusive for the child. This is because the child is experiencing things beyond his or her ability to cope with emotionally at that age level.

Sexual abuse can be either physical, in which there is actual bodily contact between the abuser and the child, or nonphysical. One special nonphysical form of emotional sexual abuse occurs when a parent has a relationship with a child of the opposite sex that is more important to the parent than the relationship with the spouse.

PHYSICAL SEXUAL ABUSE

Physical sexual abuse is bodily sexual activity with a child or touching in a sexual way. This includes intercourse, oral sex, anal sex, an adult masturbating a child or having a child masturbate an adult, and sexual hugging, sexual kissing, and sexual touching (known as fondling). When any of these are done by a family member the abuse is called *incest*; when done by a nonfamily member they're called *child molestation*.

IS IT STILL ABUSIVE IF THE SEXUAL ENCOUNTER DIDN'T HURT?

As "human animals" we are designed to respond to sexual stimulation starting at birth. And some forms of sexual abuse actually feel very good to a child. If a child is fondled, for instance, it may not cause pain; it may in fact feel wonderful to the child. The fact that the fondling felt good or even that a child asked for it still does not mean the *child* is responsible for being sexual with an adult. It is the *adult* who is out of control. In fact, when I'm dealing with an adult who has been victimized by an act of sexual abuse that felt good, this person is more difficult to treat, because he or she wants to take responsibility for allowing the sexual activity to happen or letting it continue to happen.

Little children do not naturally seek out sexual encounters beyond what is normal for their age levels. The things that children who have not been abused and who are near the same age (within four years of each other) will do to one another sexually are almost always within normal range for their age and won't be experienced as traumatic (e.g., showing each other their genitals and asking questions about how the other goes to the bathroom). But if one of the children has been exposed to more adultlike sexual behavior and repeats it with the other child, it becomes sexual abuse.

Also sometimes younger children can wind up abusing older children. I was working with a man to whom nobody had said this. It took a long time before the story of the abuse came out, but he experienced incest from his two younger sisters when he was ten and they were eight and younger. They were huge and outweighed him. He carried an extra load of anguish because they were younger and he thought that he, being older, was the abuser somehow.

ARE CHILDREN EVER THE CAUSE OF THEIR OWN SEXUAL ABUSE?

A child is *never* the responsible party for adult-child sexual abuse. There are many underlying dynamics going on in a sexually abusive situation, and those dynamics concern the offending adult's lack of control.

A child is first attacked or introduced into sexual behaviors by an adult or older child, so whatever knowledge a child has of sexual behavior beyond his or her age level has been learned through inappropriate encounters with someone else. Later on, if the child has been very seriously abused, it will appear that he or she is setting the abuse up by instigating it, but even that behavior has been taught to the child during earlier abuse experiences and is therefore not his or her fault.

For example, some children receive very little or no appropriate physical nurturing from a caregiver. If such a child is sexually abused in a manner that feels good and thereby experiences the much-needed physical touching, the child will seek out that sexual touching because he or she has such a strong need for physical contact. The child is actually starved for physical attention and seeks out sexual contact— not because of its sexual nature but because of the deep need for physical touch the child will do anything to get. The child is driven by his or her own internal need toward nurturing physical contact and substitutes sexual contact for it. Such a child on the surface appears to be the perpetrator of the sexual activity with an adult but actually is not—the child is merely trying to get his or her physical nurturing needs met. Since the child has not experienced any appropriate physical nurturing, he or she doesn't know that there is any other way to meet this need for physical nurturing.

A woman I'll call Celeste always comes to mind when I think of multiple incest. This patient was the victim of incest from fifteen males before she was eight, all of whom were older adult males in her family. Both of her parents were gutter drunks and were flagrantly abusive in ways other than sex. Her food, clothing, and shelter were uncertain and in some sense were up for grabs on a daily basis.

But Uncle Harry would come over every night, starting when Celeste was eight years old, and masturbate her and have her masturbate him. To Celeste this was wonderful. Uncle Harry was her friend and made her feel good.

At that time she learned to confuse physical nurturing with sexual experiences. Later she confused emotional and intellectual nurturing with them. Celeste learned that whenever she was lonely and needed nurturing, she could only get that closeness in her world by engaging in sexual acts. And before long Celeste was a sex addict. Part of her therapy involved trying to teach her that compulsive sexual activity will not meet her needs for physical and emotional nurturing.

It was very difficult to help Celeste because she "loved" Uncle Harry a lot and the sexual experiences he had given her felt especially good because of what she *wasn't* getting in the way of appropriate nurturing. So we taught her that physical nurturing will take care of some of her need, emotional nurturing will take care of other parts of it, and intellectual nurturing will take care of still other parts of it. We taught her how to seek, receive, and give these kinds of nurturing rather than only seeking sexual stimulation and sexual intimacy when she felt needy and isolated.

We taught her to seek these various kinds of nonsexual nurturing from other people who were appropriate and safe. Part of her therapy was teaching her how to ask for hugs from safe people instead of trying to be sexual with everybody. She had to learn to be physical but appropriate and nonsexual and how to share feelings and then listen to feelings coming back from another person, so she could be emotionally intimate and get some emotional nourishment.

Any adult who continues to use a child's need for physical contact to draw the child into having sexual encounters is offering inappropriate physical nurturing and abusing that child. And as I said earlier this is true even if the child seeks out and seems to enjoy these encounters.

Often in therapy patients will not say anything about the abusive sex feeling good for a long time, until they really trust the therapist. And when they do tell, these patients often have profound shame and guilt. They feel so guilty because they felt an intense "positive" drive toward the person sexually abusing them, a drive that was within them only as a result of *not experiencing appropriate physical nurturing*. I look for this when I meet a lot of resistance from a client to looking at sexual abuse.

My guideline here is: whenever an adult is sexual with a child, the child is experiencing sexual abuse. It is never ultimately brought about by the child's instigation. Sexual abuse is *always* the responsibility of the adult and is about his or her sex addiction or lack of sexual boundaries.

It's sad to me to have to say that many therapists still tend to blame the child for getting sexually abused if the child is willing or instigates the sexual contact. In fact, while I was presenting a workshop recently a therapist talked to me in a blaming way about "a child allowing abuse to happen" and "setting herself up to be abused." That is what I call an "offender statement"— a statement by an adult blaming a child for abuse received at the hands of an adult. The child has not developed boundaries and needs protection, not blame, from adults. If you're ever working with a therapist who makes that kind of blaming statement to you, my advice would be to find another therapist. The therapist very likely does not know how to approach sexual abuse.

SEXUAL PLAY OR ABUSE?

Sexual abuse is almost always done to a child by an adult or an older child. But sometimes a same-age or younger child who has been sexually abused by an older person may turn around and act out that same abusive behavior on another child.

A rough rule of thumb for distinguishing between normal sexual play and sexual abuse is this: if a child is experiencing sexual activity at the hands of a child who is four or more years older or from a child who has been taught sexual behavior beyond his or her age level, it is likely that sexual abuse is happening.

WHEN PHYSICAL SEXUAL ABUSE IS EMPOWERING

Physical-sexual abuse that doesn't hurt can be very empowering; it arouses children, and in the sexual arousal and orgasm, if it happens, their bodies feel a flood of exhilarating energy. When children experience incest from a parent and are taught that they are meeting the offender's sexual needs much better than the other parent, the implication is that they *are* better and more sexually potent than the most important same-sex adult in this child's life.

The most typical form of this is called "Daddy's little girl." The father tells his daughter that Mom won't be sexual with him. Then he sexually abuses the daughter without hurting her physically; it sexually arouses her so that she feels very good. She gets the idea, "I'm better than Mom because I'm being sexual with Dad. I am wonderful. I am great."

Experiencing the physical flood of energy, making the parent feel really good, and being so important to the parent give these incest victims a sense of tremendous power and superiority, although it is false of course in that they are not superior, but have value equal to everyone else. In such cases the fact that these sexual experiences are abusive is masked, because they don't hurt.

OVERT NONPHYSICAL SEXUAL ABUSE

Overt nonphysical sexual abuse can affect people as profoundly as direct physical touching and involves two different kinds of sexual behavior: voyeurism ("peeping") and exhibitionism ("flashing"). Voyeurism and exhibitionism by family members can sometimes hurt a child much more than when done by someone outside the family.

Voyeurism happens when a family member gets sexually stimulation from looking at another family member. (This of course does not include appropriate sexual interaction between husband and wife.) *Exhibitionism* is taking place when a family member is being sexually stimulated by exposing the sexual parts of his or her body to the child. Several years ago flashing was considered very funny and comedians made a great thing of it. But flashing and voyeurism are associated with what Patrick Carnes calls "level two sex addiction."*

Our culture has a way of giving us the message that we're not to talk about sex addiction, yet it's very blatant and much more common than many people realize. And when examples of sex addiction are going on around us, we tend to laugh about them and think they're funny or normal. Their results are not funny.

When I ask people whether they experienced voyeurism or exhibitionism, I suggest that they try to remember its happening both outside and inside their family. I think it is easier to understand the abusive nature of some adult male driving up and saying, "Hey, little girl, look at me," and flashing his genitals or having a "peeping Tom" outside one's bathroom or bedroom window. But when these things are done within the family, they often aren't identified as abusive. When voyeurism or exhibitionism by older family members occurs, the person engaging in the behavior is still sexually stimulating himself or herself at the expense of the child's sexual/emotional well-being. This is serious sexual abuse, even though there's no hands-on touching or any conscious intent on the part of the adult to "harm" the child.

In these families people are often nude in each other's presence, and members routinely leer at the other members' bodies. The attitude about privacy in such a family sends a message to the child something like this: "Nobody is to be private. If you're private you're a prude. There are no closed doors to the bathroom or the bedrooms. Everybody should see everybody. And if you feel shamed and don't like this, it means *you* have a problem. It doesn't mean that I'm out of control."

The factor that makes exhibitionism and voyeurism different from a lack of sexual boundaries is that in exhibitionism or voyeurism the offender intends to get sexually stimulated. In other families the

---

*Patrick Carnes, *Out of the Shadows: Understanding Sexual Addiction* (Minneapolis, MN: Comp Care, 1983), pp. 37–45.

same degree of nudity may happen, but the adults are just careless about sexual boundaries, which we will see in a few paragraphs can also be sexually abusive *to the child*.

Children who experience acts of voyeurism and exhibitionism are often not sure if such acts went on in the family or not. Here's how this kind of situation might seem to someone trying to remember.

Christine is an adult who came in for therapy. As I talked to her about voyeurism and exhibitionism, she wasn't sure but she had the feeling that this behavior could possibly have gone on. When she thought back about what happened in her family, she remembered having a sense that when she was dressing or undressing, trying to go to the bathroom or take a shower, or in her bedroom doing private things, she wasn't safe. She had the sense that her father was going to come in and look at her or try to expose himself to her. She remembered having thoughts like, "Oh, here comes Dad. I don't like seeing him nude." It's as if there were some energy Dad was giving off that felt unusual and overwhelming. But she didn't realize there was anything wrong with her father's behavior at the time, because children don't understand about that kind of sexual energy or out-of-control sexual behavior. Sometimes there is just an uneasy feeling about having seen the parents nude or having the parents see them nude or only partially dressed.

COVERT NONPHYSICAL SEXUAL ABUSE

Covert sexual abuse is indirect, manipulative, and hidden and the offender does not usually do it for the purpose of sexual stimulation. One kind of covert sexual abuse is verbal and the other is related to boundaries.

VERBAL SEXUAL ABUSE

One expression of verbal sexual abuse is inappropriate sexual talk in the family—sexual innuendos, sexual joking, sexual name calling, and grilling kids after a date for sexual information. Perhaps the father tells sexual jokes that are far beyond a child's sexual development and are in any case not appropriate for a dad to be telling a child. Or the father in anger might call his daughter a whore.

When parents grill teenagers after a date about the specific nature of their sexual behavior (which is none of their business), they shame them, whether or not anything overtly sexual had taken place during the date. Appropriate sex education is a natural part of the child's being taught about life, but to try to ferret out "what happened" after the fact, disregarding the son's or daughter's right to privacy, is a shaming experience. In a more functional family a relationship of trust has been established and shame has not been attached to the subject of sex, so functional children often use early dating experiences as occasions to ask questions to which the parent can respond in a way that is healthy and not emotionally loaded.

Verbal sexual abuse also goes on when a parent acts like he or she would like to be in a romantic relationship with the child. Perhaps the father tells his daughter that he would like to date her if only he were younger. He may talk about how nicely formed her body is and how he wished he could "get a little of it." Or he may make lewd remarks about her body, like mention how big her breasts are. Or a mother might make sexually loaded comments about how large a son's muscles or genitals are, and so on.

Another aspect to verbal sexual abuse has to do with sexual information. First of all, I believe all children need information about sexuality. Our sexuality is a very powerful drive, and reproduction for the continuation of the human race depends on babies being born into families where they can be cared for. But some babies get tragically conceived and born to young, inexperienced mothers who are not prepared to care for them. And a major reason is the lack of adequate sexual information.

But the point is that our sexual drive is extremely powerful. Our children need information about their sexual development, sexual drive and about what constitutes appropriate sexual behavior and sexual expectations not only to avoid unwanted pregnancy but also to protect themselves from possible emotional trauma that often surrounds this powerful yet sensitive part of our lives.

At one extreme, it is abusive not to give children any information about sex, expecting them to get it from their peers or the school. I support school sex education programs that give sexual information to children, but since there is such a wide range of attitudes about appropriate sexuality, information about sexual behavior should come from parents as well as teachers and peers.

At the other extreme, it is abusive to give children too much information about sex or tell them too early. It is also abusive to give them jaded, skewed, or false sexual information, such as telling a girl she will get pregnant if she kisses a boy on the mouth, that the reason kids have pimples is because they're masturbating, or that masturbation is evil and sinful.

Masturbation is part of normal development. It is how we keep our brain, which is our master sex gland, connected to our genitals, which is one of the main places we experience sexual stimulation. Masturbation helps us become sexually functional adults. It's completely inappropriate to tell a child that masturbating is abnormal. A functional parent is concerned only if the child is masturbating obsessively and compulsively or hurting or distressing himself or herself. Otherwise it's nobody's business whether the child is masturbating. In fact, the child needs both privacy and the knowledge that masturbating is a part of normal sexual development. Telling a child not to masturbate can set the child up to become obsessed with it. It's like my telling you not to think about monkeys for ten minutes. Can you do it? All the time you're trying not to think about monkeys you're going to be concentrating on monkeys. And of course there is no primary life force predisposing us to think about monkeys.

I'll never forget one fearful situation in my life caused by my own lack of sexual information. When I was in fourth grade several of us who were close girlfriends were sitting around in a group after school. One of the girls had been digging around in her parents' room and found some condoms, and she was trying to tell the rest of us what they were for. By the time she stopped talking I was petrified. First of all, my parents had never told me *anything* about sex. I was totally repulsed by what she said and stayed that way until I was in high school.

SEXUAL BOUNDARIES

When children are raised in a dysfunctional family system in which the parents do not have appropriate sexual boundaries, they grow up without them themselves, even though there is no intent to abuse. Examples of behavior by parents with inadequate boundaries include being sexual with the door open so that the children can hear or see what the parents are doing, or closing the door but making so much noise during sexual intercourse that the children can hear through the walls and vents. They French kiss in the kitchen and fondle each other on the living room couch. These are not examples of exhibitionism because the parents do not need the children's attention to become sexually aroused. The parents are just careless about keeping their physical intimacy private and protecting the children from their adult sexuality.

Such parents are also likely to appear in their underwear or naked in front of the child. Again, this isn't "flashing," because the parents aren't doing it for sexual stimulation; they are just being careless about protecting the child from their adult nudity. The parents may enter the bathroom when the child is taking a shower—they may not be voyeurs but they are disrespecting the child's right to privacy.

There is no harm intended in such situations, but these examples do *not* teach the child to develop intact sexual boundaries. It's just part of the tragedy of dysfunctional family systems that they reproduce themselves in succeeding generations, unless there is some sort of interruption through a recovery process.

If each parent has a different kind of dysfunctional boundary, the child, on becoming an adult, may alternate between the two types of sexual boundary systems. For example, Gary grows up in a home in which his mother has a wall of fear for a sexual boundary. She avoids sex by hiding her body and keeping her distance from her husband. But Gary's father has no sexual boundaries at all. He's very open about discussing sex, telling sexual jokes, and walking around the house nude, and barging into Gary's sister's bedroom and ogling her when she's dressing. As an adult Gary vascillates between doing inappropriate sexual things and hiding and avoiding sex altogether out of fear.

The way appropriate sexual boundaries are established in a functional family is that the parents demonstrate their own boundaries. They teach their children to stay out of the parents' bedroom or the bathroom while the parents are dressing or using the toilet. They also teach the children to have privacy when they are using the toilet, bathing, or dressing. Of course, in the beginning a child needs assistance in learning to go to the bathroom, bathe, and dress. But as soon as the children can do these things on their own, they are allowed to do them alone with the door open. Later on they are asked to shut the door, and still later they are taught to shut and lock it. From then on the children know that this is appropriate wherever they are.

After the children are a certain age, functional parents do not run around the house nude or in their underwear. I personally believe this age line is reached when the child is old enough to be clearly aware of the physical sexual difference between mother and father—about age four or five. Functional parents also don't allow their children to sleep with them.

I am not saying that there is something wrong with nudity. When I refer to protecting children from it, I mean this: when children reach a certain age they begin to notice that Mom and Dad are different and start focusing on those sexual differences. It's easy for adults to forget that when a child is little and they look up at Mom and Dad, everything looks even larger than it actually is. When a child looks at the size of adult genitalia and breasts and then compares his or her own little body, it can be very frightening, overwhelming, and shaming.

Of course, if a child accidentally walks into a room where a parent is naked, it would not be appropriate for the parent to be angry and dive behind a dresser as if there were something wrong with his or her nude body. But the parent could cover himself or herself and ask the child to wait outside the room until the parent is dressed.

In addition to that, as a child ages and starts producing hormones, he or she gets directly interested in sex and sexuality. If the parents continue to go around nude, it won't be unusual for the child to start getting sexually stimulated by looking at the parents' nude bodies.

For example, twelve-year-old Douglas has started having erections, masturbating, thinking a lot about girls, telling sexual jokes at school, and so on. His mother, while sitting in the bathtub, calls to him and says, "Hey Doug, come in here. I want to talk to you." She sincerely just wants to talk to him (not "flash" him), but her naked body is exposed. So Douglas comes in and sits down on the toilet lid, looks at her in the bathtub, notices her breasts, and starts getting an erection. The mother does not intend to stimulate her son into an erection, but nevertheless calling him into the bathroom while she is exposed in the bathtub is inappropriate and its results are highly abusive.

While a very young child may easily get overwhelmed by the size of same-sex parent's adult nude body, when the child gets older, protection may not be so great a concern. If an older child is physically developing and feeling adequate, and if you have a good relationship, it usually isn't a negative thing for a mother and daughter or father and son to be together in their underwear, dressing together in the same room, or talking in the bathroom with one of them in the shower. Parents have to use their good judgment in these kinds of situations.

For example, I have a twenty-four-year-old daughter and I don't worry about that kind of thing with her. We can dress in the same room without feeling self-conscious. But no matter what age my sons are (the youngest is eleven), I would never be around them undressed or in the bathtub.

I realize that there are no "standard rules" in this area and that some of the opinions I've expressed may be considered arbitrary. But what I'm trying to point out is that sexually abusive practices have been passed down for so many generations in some families that they are now considered "normal" to both parents and children. But my clinical experience indicates that much nudity and carelessness regarding sexual boundaries is very shaming and abusive and leads to dysfunction in the child's adult life.

EMOTIONAL SEXUAL ABUSE

Children's sexual development involves sexual identity, preferred sources of affection, and sexual preference. Sexual identity is learning about what it means to be a person of your sex. A female learns, "How am I feminine?" A male learns, "How am I masculine?" Children also learn from whom they prefer to get affection or nonsexual physical nurturing—men or women. Later, a man can prefer to be around other men in this way or he can prefer to be around nurturing women. A woman can prefer nurturing men or she can prefer other women for hugging, holding, or touching in a nonsexual way. *Sexual preference* is learning and embracing which gender we find to be sexually stimulating.

The kind of abuse I am about to describe is emotionally abusive because it tries to force the children into being adults. It's sexually abusive because it creates a great deal of confusion about sexual identity, preferences for affection, and direct sexual behavior.

One of the benchmark criteria for distinguishing a dysfunctional family system from a functional one is that within a functional family system, the adults are there as parents to meet the needs of the children. In a dysfunctional family, the children are there to meet the needs of the adults. Emotional sexual abuse is one of the most glaring examples of children being used to meet the needs of the parents.

In a functional family there is a boundary between the two parents on one hand and all the children on the other. This external and internal boundary system protects the children from the very intimate details of the relationship between the parents. The children need to know only about 80 percent of what's going on between the parents. The rest of it is none of their business.

In the accompanying diagram of a functional family, the Xs represent the parents, the line represents the boundary, and the Os represent the children. The parents relate to each other intimately yet demonstrate a proper boundary between their relationship with each other and their relationship with the children.

A FUNCTIONAL FAMILY

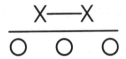

Parents Relate to Each Other,
Boundary Protects Children

Emotional sexual abuse occurs when one parent has a relationship with a child that is more important to that parent than the relationship with the spouse. In effect, the child is drawn up through the boundary and placed between the parents in their intimate world.

The parent who has entered such a relationship with a child is (consciously or unconsciously) asking the child to meet the parent's emotional needs either for affection or for a romantic relationship with someone of the opposite sex; in a functional family these needs would be met by the other spouse. This sort of abusive relationship usually results from the fact that the parents are having trouble being intimate and meeting each other's needs. Two codependent parents who have been abused themselves usually do not know how to be intimate in an adult relationship. One may try to respond to this lack of ability by getting in a close relationship with a child

A DYSFUNCTIONAL FAMILY

Children Are Drawn into the Parents' Intimate World

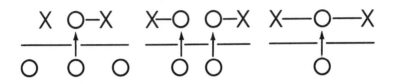

A. One parent relates primarily to one child

B. Both parents relate primarily to different children

C. Both parents relate primarily to same child

rather than trying to relate to the other spouse. Such a parent is inappropriately emotionally intimate with the child.

Often the parent in this kind of relationship will tell the child many or all of the intimate details of the marriage relationship, how bad it is, how it's not working, and what a "jerk" the other spouse is. The child becomes an emotional dumping ground for feelings the parent does not want to deal with. This sort of relating also damages the child's relationship with the other parent. And to such a child the idea of marriage in general can overwhelm the child with pain and shame.

This sort of abuse is extremely common when there is an addict in the family. One example is a family in which the father is an addict and the mother is an identified codependent. Dad is an alcoholic, often off drinking, a work addict, working almost all the time, or perhaps a sex addict, having many affairs with other women. Whatever the addiction, he is doing something away from the family and is almost never home to be intimate with Mom. So Mom winds up being emotionally intimate with one (or more) of her children and using that child as an intimate adult companion. In another scenario the mother is the addict with a special relationship to a child who takes care of the father and the other children for her.

Sometimes the dynamics work a little differently. Two children can be drawn up into the relationship between the parents (see example B in the diagram). The father draws one in and the mother takes the other. When this happens, the relationship between those two children is like World War III, because the emotional problems that aren't dealt with directly between the parents are often fought out by the kids.

Sometimes two codependent parents both have this "special" kind of relationship with an only child (see example C). This makes that child feel crazy, but also powerful. He or she is the central figure and confidant in the family, often a "double agent" in the family drama.

When the "special" experience is between a mother and a daughter, the daughter is known as Mom's confidant, Mom's caretaker, or family caretaker in Mom's place. When it's between mother and son, he's known as Mommy's little man, Mommy's surrogate husband, or Mama's boy. When it's father-daughter, she's known as Daddy's little girl, Daddy's little princess, or surrogate wife. When it's father and son, the son is known as Daddy's confidant, Daddy's caretaker, or family caretaker in Dad's place.

The father-son example might be hard to see. Usually what happens is that both parents are relating to the son (as in example C). The son meets the father's needs by taking care of Mom for Dad. The father's message is, "You take care of me by standing in for me. I'm working hard (a work addict) and I'm too busy. You take care of the family while I'm gone."

Children aren't supposed to take care of the family or even the other children—that is the job of the parents. Children are supposed to do the developmental tasks of each age level or "be busy being kids." When a parent expects the child to take care of the family (or any one person in it), the child does not get to have a childhood.

As a therapist, I have found that people who have experienced this kind of abuse are often confused as adults about sexual identity, affectional comfort, and sexual preference. Sexual preference issues get blurred more often as a result of physical sexual abuse however. For example, if a young boy is sexually abused by his coach, he may think "If I attracted a man to abuse me, maybe I'm homosexual," when in fact, he is not. It was the preference of the coach that led him to choose the boy as his victim, not the sexual preference of the boy, himself, but the boy is still confused about his sexual preference as a result.

When a parent requires adult intimacy from a child, it isn't unusual for the other parent to hate the child who is having the relationship with the spouse. Or if Mom keeps telling her daughter that Dad is horrible, terrible, and unsafe, the child has difficulty relaxing and letting a man (any man) hug her. It won't be safe. Although her sexual energy might propel her in adulthood to be sexual with a man, her emotional sexual abuse issues might make her prefer to get non-sexual physical nurturing only from women. Also the daughter will probably have trouble liking Dad (who is so "mean" to Mom) and will act that out, so then Dad won't like her. Either way, the daughter is cut off from the love that should be coming to her from her father and this can affect her adult relationships with men.

My mother sexually abused me this way. She was a chemical addict and my dad was emotionally absent and offensive. As a child, I thought Dad's emotional absence and attacks were all his problem and not any of Mother's. I was deluded about my Mom's drug addiction. So I would stay home and take care of her. And my dad kept giving me the message that I was inadequate and worthless. The message said that my being female meant that I was of less value and that when I did anything feminine I was worthless. This set up some confusion for me about my identity as a woman.

When I grew up, I could not demonstrate my own femininity. I dressed in a drab way and had a hairstyle with nothing feminine about it at all that made me blend into the walls. Later on I had trouble learning how to dress and be feminine. I thought exhibiting feminine traits was stupid and that I was smarter than to want to dress in a feminine way. I had no idea that I was being very dysfunctional.

One of the issues in my recovery is learning how to be female. First of all I'm working on looking like a female. It was dreadfully painful learning how to go to the store and shop. It's a major miracle when I can wear big earrings because I know that will attract attention to my face. Before, I didn't want anyone to look at it. So for me, and thousands of others, emotional sexual abuse is very harmful and presents difficult issues for recovery.

I think one of the most difficult sexual abuse positions to be in is to be "Daddy's little girl." Although this is changing, men are usually more powerful than women, and to be Daddy's little girl and be more important to Daddy than Mommy is probably the most highly seductive experience in our culture. Such a woman compares every man she's with to her daddy and usually cannot find a man who could ever be what Daddy was to her. In addition, she has great difficulty growing up and sometimes remains a "little girl" emotionally all her life. It's her little girl behavior that seduces men, and she keeps expecting the man in her life to respond to her as her daddy did. A healthy man won't do that, although he might go crazy trying to get this woman to hold up her end of the relationship and "be there" for him as an adult would.

It is especially tragic if Daddy's little girl marries an incest perpetrator. She has her babies, then her husband seduces their daughter and the mother lives out the scenario from the other side. Her daughter is in an incestuous relationship with her husband, and the mother winds up hating her own daughter just as her mother hated her. And it goes on and on. Why? Because that's all she knows. She doesn't have a sexual boundary to even indicate to her that all this behavior is dysfunctional, even though at one level she may be angry or even horrified at the unfairness of it all.

EMOTIONAL SEXUAL ABUSE CAN BE DISEMPOWERING OR EMPOWERING

Emotional sexual abuse can be *disempowering* when the child tries to meet the parent's expectations to take care of the parent in this special relationship, but realizes that he or she lacks the skills to do it.

But emotional sexual abuse is often *empowering*. When "Daddy's little girl" or "Mom's little man" gets taken out on "dates" by the opposite sex parent such as to the movies or out to dinner, the child starts to believe, "I am the center of Dad's (or Mom's) attention and I am better than Mom (or Dad)." There's nothing wrong with a father paying attention to his daughter and taking her out to dinner or to a movie (or mother a son), but when these actions are accompanied by verbal messages that the child is more fun than Mom (or Dad) or better than Mom (or Dad)—when it is plain to the child that the parent prefers him or her to the other parent—empowering abuse is taking place.

This can happen with a single parent who prefers the child's company to that of an adult of the opposite sex and tells the child so. Sexual needs and the need for companionship from the opposite sex are meant to be met on an adult-to-adult level. When a parent seeks and gets that need met from a child, whether or not any physical sexual contact takes place, he or she is abusing that child.

When a potentially empowering situation happens (from direct physical sexual abuse as with incest, or from emotional sexual abuse) and the other parent confronts it, even by being angry at or shaming the child, the child gets disempowered. But more often the "left out" spouse is very much a victim, does not see the abuse going on, and wouldn't know how to confront it if he or she did.

Another possibility for empowerment is when the spouse condones the abuse through his or her own dysfunctional behavior. Perhaps the mother is disinterested in her husband, repelled by him, or afraid of him, and is glad to let this daughter fill in for her. In this situation both parents are glad the daughter is playing this role in the family. But the effect on the *child* is still abusive, even though both parents agree about the intimate relationship of the child with one parent.

This empowering kind of abuse creates children who grow up to be offenders who believe they have the right to take from other people. There is no apparent experience of the shame core because they never got shamed.

As we've seen, sexual abuse is much broader and more complex than most people think. And years later the effects of abuse on a child in this area of family life make the adult codependent's journey toward recovery very difficult.

CHAPTER 12

Emotional Abuse

Emotional abuse is probably the most frequent kind of abuse. It happens through verbal abuse, social abuse, and the neglect or abandonment of dependency needs.

VERBAL ABUSE

Verbal abuse occurs when the parent attacks the child verbally, screaming, calling the child names, or using sarcasm or ridicule. It is probably one of the most intense forms of emotional abuse.

When parents *scream* at their children they attack their delicate little ears. Most children want to hear their parents, but not if they are screaming. When a parent starts screaming, children often close their ears down and *can't* hear, which is a natural survival mechanism. Remember, to small children the parents are huge and powerful, and hearing the parents scream is frightening. In a dysfunctional family, often the next thing the parents do after screaming is attack the children physically because they "weren't listening."

Name calling added to screaming makes verbal abuse even more harmful. My name is "Pia." It's not "asshole," it's not "fatso," it's not "whore," it's not "stupid." It's "Pia." When somebody calls me by my name and treats me with respect, I get the sense that I'm precious. When I hear a derogatory name, I don't.

Ridiculing, or making fun of, children is done by parents who I believe are discharging anger in an indirect way. When children are ridiculed they have no defense, no way to avoid feeling bad about themselves, especially when they are very young.

Listening to verbal abuse being done to someone else can be just as abusive as watching physical or sexual abuse done to someone else. Children do not have well-developed boundaries. Even if they "know" the tirade is not directed at them, they still feel almost as much impact as if it were.

There are a number of "soundproof" rooms at The Meadows in which therapy groups meet. These rooms are soundproofed with thick insulation to try to cut down the noise when people are doing Gestalt and shame reduction work, which may involve angry screaming, crying, and other loud noises. The insulation was put in because some patients who had been verbally abused as children became extremely upset and even had shame attacks or experienced spontaneous regressions just listening to the sounds that come through the vents. This shame may come from having listened to a parent scream at a family member in the listener's childhood.

SOCIAL ABUSE

In the early stages of life, children learn who they are and how to do things (such as get dressed, make a telephone call, and so on) from their parents. Between the ages of four and six, children's friends become extremely important, because they also teach them a lot about who they are, how to do what kids do at their own age, and how to be in relationships with other children. Social abuse happens when the parents directly or indirectly interfere with the children's access to their peers.

This interference can be done directly, by saying things like, "This family has secrets and nobody's to come in here to find them out." Or, "We don't air our dirty linen in public. No, you can't have your friends over. It's not safe with outsiders. Just stay with us; we're all you need. And, no, you can't go to anybody's house."

Indirect abuse occurs when the children just don't have the freedom to let their friends into their home to enjoy them. Examples include the parents' being so out of control with their own addictions that the children have to stay home and cook and clean and don't have time to be with their peers. And even if the parents don't say, "Keep other kids out," the children wouldn't bring friends home under any circumstances because of what might happen if they did. Maybe Dad's an alcoholic and the children never know when he'll be drunk on the living room couch when they come home. If Dad's a sex addict, he might try to fondle the children's female friends. Perhaps it's Mom who tries to hustle her daughter's boyfriends when the daughter brings them home. Or Dad might be a rage addict and the children never know when he's going to slap or punch them, or verbally ridicule them, which he sometimes does in front of other people.

An unusual handicap or physical or mental illness may also cause a problem. For instance, if Mom is in a wheelchair she might give the indirect (or direct) message, "Don't embarrass me by bringing your friends home." In a functional family the children are helped to adjust to mom's physical handicap and told that Mom feels fine about having the children's friends around (if she does). Such a family even helps the children know what to say to their friends' questions about the wheelchair.

NEGLECT AND ABANDONMENT

Of all the kinds of abuse, neglect and abandonment are the ones that may need to be looked at the most in our culture, especially by codependents having trouble piecing together their history.

I approach abuse due to neglect and abandonment from two perspectives. One is to find out how well the patient's dependency needs were met when he or she was a child. The other is to look at addictions operating in the major caregivers and the role these addictions played in neglect and/or abandonment of the patient as a child.

Dependency needs include the need for:

Food	Physical nurturing
Clothing	Emotional nurturing (time, attention,
Shelter	and direction)
Medical/dental care	Sexual guidance and information
	Financial guidance and information

When any one of these dependency needs is neglected or ignored, children experience abuse. Emotional nurturing is especially important for children to develop toward maturity. When children's emotional nurturing needs are met by the parents, they learn who they are in a positive way. Functional parents say to the children—automatically and nonverbally—"you're worthwhile." Emotional nurturing also teaches the children "how to do things" the family's way. Children have to get a sense of how to process information and approach the tasks of living; receiving this information and "know-how" is a vital need. Once we've seen that emotional damage is the basis for the rest of the codependent condition, it is easy to see that having this need met is absolutely crucial for children.

Neglect means that these needs for emotional nurturing were not met well enough and the children were shamed. For instance, if a father doesn't teach a son how to be a man and do the things a man is supposed to do about work, money, clothes, and relationships with men and women, the son feels inadequate and experiences shame in the face of his ignorance about these things. In most cases of neglect, there was some attempt made at giving the children emotional nurturing; it just wasn't enough.

With *abandonment* these emotional nurturing needs simply were not met. It happens when one or both parents are not available to the children. One or both may by physically removed from the home or they may be physically present, but emotionally removed. Children can be abandoned within the home when they are ignored because of parents' preoccupation with other things or people.

Abandonment can happen as a result of divorce. A parent

moves away and may come back for visits and send money through the mail for food, clothing, shelter, and medical care, but he or she isn't there to physically nurture or to give the children time, attention, and direction.

Sometimes parents actually do feel overwhelmed with the caretaking of their children either consciously or unconsciously. They may think sending them away to boarding school at an early age is the answer. But being sent away from home at a young age can be less than nurturing even though the parent does not intend it to be, because the children do not get time, attention, and direction *from the parent*, except on short visits home.

Abandonment can happen through a death due to illness or accident. Also, if a parent commits suicide, threatens suicide, or attempts it but survives, the children can have a profound abandonment issue to deal with. Abandonment can happen because a parent actually does physically abandon the home. It may be that when the children get up one morning, Mom or Dad has disappeared. There could be many repeated abandonments by one or the other parent.

A good friend of mine whose mother had seven children talked to me about being abandoned by her mother on a routine basis. When any of the children expressed a need for attention and care from her, she'd go out of control and beat them, primarily with a high-heeled shoe. And when that wouldn't make things go the way she thought they should, she'd pack her suitcases, walk out the door and not come back for two or three days at a time. The children were left alone until their father got home from work and took care of them.

ADDICTIONS CAUSE ABANDONMENT AND NEGLECT

Addictions such as chemical dependency (drug addiction or alcoholism); sex addiction; compulsive gambling; religious addiction; eating disorders; compulsive spending; work addiction; and love addiction can cause parents to neglect or abandon their children.

Love addiction is a requirement for the positive regard (called "love") of a significant "other" in order for one to be comfortable and "stable." The love addict is willing to do anything, no matter how harmful or humiliating to the self, to gain that positive regard, and experiences a painful, unbalanced state of "withdrawal" when that positive regard is not forthcoming. A person can be in a love addiction with another adult, one's parent, or one's own child. If a parent is love-addicted to someone, the parent's obsessive focus on the object of that addiction leads to neglect and abandonment of the children. Even if a child is the object of such addiction, the true needs and wants of the child are overlooked.*

Work addiction—being "too busy" with projects, whether at a job or around the house, hobbies, repairs, and so on to relate to others—is just as offensive and destructive to children's development as any of these other addictions, but it's harder to deal with because our culture supports it. Yet if the father or mother is a work addict, children's needs for emotional nurturing go unmet.

Some eating disorders can cause a parent to neglect or abandon children. A bulimic mother may be throwing up in the bathroom and not available to her children. Or if she purges through exercise, she can be gone all the time attending to her body.

Obesity often makes the parent lethargic and unable to play physically with the children. Also, the appearance of the obese parent (as with any other physical disfigurement) may shame a child. Children need to be counseled through such situations by an adult, not just expected to cope somehow.

Also, if the mother has a thin/fat eating disorder and believes that she's fat when she's not—she doesn't really "know" what her body looks like—she may very well see her children as fat and badger them about dieting and watching their weight when in fact their weight is normal. I've had people with adult eating disorders talk about the fact that they thought they were fat as children. I've asked them to

*A four-cassette lecture by Pia Mellody about addictive relationships is available from Mellody Enterprises, P.O. Box 1739, Wickenburg, AZ 85358.

bring me some pictures of themselves to see how fat they were. When they bring the pictures many of them are shocked and say, "I wasn't fat as a kid *at all*! What was my mom talking about?"

PARENTAL PHYSICAL AND MENTAL ILLNESS

Although physical and mental illness aren't addictions, their effect on the family can be the same. If a parent is mentally ill (out of touch with reality) or physically ill, that parent often isn't available emotionally, whether the parent is at home or away.

This is another case where parental intention is irrelevant. Most people don't want to be physically or mentally ill. But illness can create the same problems in the children's lives as other forms of abuse, when the parent is so ill he or she is not available to take care of the children.

PARENTAL CODEPENDENCE

As we saw in chapter 3, codependent parents may experience addictions, physical illness, or mental illness as a way to avoid reality because they cannot tolerate pain. We have just seen the issues of neglect and abandonment these can cause.

Also parental codependence can result in neglect or abandonment of children as we saw in chapter 7. Since a codependent parent has been abused before recovery begins, he or she doesn't know how to nurture children in a way that truly meets their needs. The parent proceeds along his or her dysfunctional behavioral path, knowing only how to gather other-esteem by "serving" and take care of others, often outside the family. This can happen to the extent that the parent is spread too thin and isn't available to nurture the children in his or her own family. He or she becomes drained "trying to take care of everyone." Eventually the overworked codependent may explode in anger and frustration, retreat into emotional or mental exhaustion, or withdraw and pout. Any of these reactions may result in neglect or abandonment of the children.

CHAPTER 13

Intellectual Abuse

How do functional families nurture their children intellectually? I believe they do two important things for children in the realm of intellectual development: support the children's thinking and provide a method of problem solving and a philosophy of life.

SUPPORTING THE CHILD'S THINKING

Intellectual abuse occurs whenever children's thinking is attacked or ridiculed, they are not allowed to do their own thinking, or they are not supported when their thinking differs from the parents' at any point. This often happens when the parent is so rigid there is no room for the child's ideas.

A functional family supports children's thinking by giving them the message that their ability to think is sound and complete, even though there is much that the children do not yet know. The children are also allowed to query the thinking and the ideas of the adults and their questions are treated respectfully. It doesn't mean the parents always agree with the children's thinking or vice versa. It means each individual in the family can do his or her own thinking, and it will be encouraged.

When children are thinking about opposing a rule that is valued by the family, the family does challenge that without attacking the children's worth. The children are given the clear message that they are not flawed because their thinking is limited and conclusions are sometimes incorrect due to a lack of knowledge. It's just that their thinking needs some fine tuning every now and then.

I try to allow my children's ideas to differ from mine, but they still have to follow my rules for their health and safety and for the care and maintenance of life in our home. I remember one day when I needed to get groceries and there was no one to stay at home with my son (who was eight at the time). But he didn't want to go with me; he wanted to stay home and watch cartoons. I acknowledged that he was differing and it's okay to differ, and then I said, "I hear that you want to stay and watch cartoons, but you're not old enough to stay here alone, so you're still going to go to the market with me, whether you want to go or not." I followed through and took him, but I didn't attack him and treat him as if I thought he was a creep because he didn't think the way I was thinking at that moment and want to go to the market with me.

A PHILOSOPHY OF LIFE AND PROBLEM SOLVING

Intellectual abuse also occurs when the children are not taught that having problems is normal and how to solve them. I remember what a shock it was to me to finally face the reality that life is full of problems I wasn't prepared for and they don't stop. The message to me had been, "You should already know how to solve this problem [whatever it was], so why should I bother explaining it to you? If you were okay, you'd know." I used to think that if I ever got into recovery and started being functional, my problems would stop. But in some ways they got worse, because I was more aware of what they were. Sometimes I'd say, "I wish I were as deluded as I used to be. I wasn't aware of how awful it is." But sometimes life really *is* as bad as it seems.* (I say this with tongue in cheek, because for me the benefits of being in recovery far outweigh the new consciousness of problems and the powerful feelings that surface now.)

---

*From Sheldon Kopp, *What Took You So Long*, (Palo Alto, CA: Science and Behavioral Publications, 1979).

I didn't learn to problem-solve until my husband, Pat, taught me. He probably taught me to save his own sanity, and it was a dreadful experience for both of us. But I'm so glad he knew, so that I could finally learn!

In our culture, not only are we adults supposed to be calm and "above it all," but the strong implication is that good, smart, successful people don't have problems. Beside telling the children that having problems is normal, the functional family provides a system of problem solving to teach the child how to approach problems and work them through.

In a dysfunctional family the parents either jump into the children's decision-making process and make the decisions for them, or they back away totally and leave the children on their own to make do with whatever immature and incomplete solutions they can come up with. When children aren't given any functional problem-solving techniques or the ones given are antisocial or skewed, then the children are being intellectually abused. If children are taught that the way to problem-solve is to "prevail" over other people no matter what, even if you have to lie, cheat, and steal, then they are taught how to be antisocial and are likely to get in a lot of trouble as adults.

One of my philosophical maxims is, "I believe that life isn't always fair." So when my children start whining and saying "life's not fair," I say, "Yeah it isn't, is it?" And we start talking about how life isn't fair at the moment.

Or they come to me and say about some personal or social situation they are in, "This is horrible. I can't stand it."

And I say, "Yes you can. After all, it's only pain and you can stand your own pain."

They look at me and admit, "Well, yeah that's true."

And I say, "Beside that, sometimes things really are as bad as they seem. And this is one of those times. I agree, this is awful. And you know what? Sometimes there's no solution even to a problem like this. All you can do is just let got of it and take care of yourself the best way you can. Here are some things you can do to take care of yourself." And then I tell them some specific things they can do.

This is what I consider appropriately teaching my children using my own philosophy of life. Everyone may not agree with my philosophy, but as a parent I need to present the best one I have discovered for myself to my children. I believe parents need to dialogue with their children, talking to each child about his or her life and the difficulties he or she faces.

NOT TELLING CHILDREN ABOUT DOUBTS

Intellectual abuse also occurs when parents do not share their own doubts about their own ideas and beliefs with their children. When parents don't share their doubts as well as their beliefs, the child has no concept that adults ever doubt or question their own beliefs. Then the children think they are supposed to have all their own ideas straight and never have any doubts about what they believe. This gets into spiritual abuse, which is the subject of the next chapter, when the parents don't share their doubts about God and their faith. These children may be stuck with feeling guilty, crazy, or unworthy whenever they have normal doubts.

Sometimes there is a fine line between the matter-of-fact statement of doubts and the dumping of the parents' fears on the children, which is not functional. But what I'm saying is that it is intellectually abusive for a parent to present himself or herself to a child as perfect, having it all together, and having no doubts or uncertainties.

CHAPTER 14

Spiritual Abuse

Spiritual abuse includes experiences that distort, retard, or otherwise interfere with a child's spiritual development. There are at least three situations in which a child may experience spiritual abuse: when a parent replaces a child's Higher Power (which happens, as we shall see in this chapter, during any kind of abuse as well as with abuse that has specific spiritual consequences); when a child's parent or parents are addicted to religion; and when a religious representative such as a minister, priest, rabbi, deacon, Sunday school teacher, or choir director abuses a child in any way.

WHEN A PARENT REPLACES A CHILD'S HIGHER POWER

When a newborn child enters a family, the parents are his or her first experience of a Higher Power—the child relies on parents for survival. Of course, people are fallible human beings and the Higher Power is not. Functional parents accept their own fallibility and are accountable for it. They convey acceptance of imperfection to their children, being accountable to the children when their fallibility harms the children, and so do not remain the child's Higher Power. Functional parents point the way to a valid Higher Power on whom they rely. For healthy spiritual development to take place, the only entity that needs to be recognized as an all-powerful, perfect being is a nonhuman, nonparental Higher Power.

The link between the physical, sexual, emotional, and intellectual forms of abuse and spiritual abuse consists of the message children get from any abuse: the abuser's attitude communicates, "I am more powerful than you. I can do whatever I want to do to you. I'm God. My will is going to prevail no matter what, and I'll abuse you to get my point across." When abusive parents put themselves in place of the Higher Power in this way in the children's lives, they model to them a punishing, self-centered, and abusive God.

Any serious abuse (such as beatings, physical sexual abuse, screaming, ridiculing, abandoning, overcontrolling, and demanding perfection) is also spiritual abuse, because it taints the child's trust of a Higher Power. Many people can never feel comfortable about God as "Father," for instance, because of the abusive father they actually had. I define a Higher Power to codependents as "a power greater than yourself and also greater than your parents."

When a parent becomes a child's Higher Power through abuse, the child comes to hate or worship that parent depending upon whether the abuse is disempowering or empowering. A child develops hate if the experience of abuse is negating, nonaffirming, violent, rejecting, judging, or blaming. This hating continues on into adulthood, and the person has a difficult time having a healthy relationship to the true Higher Power until the hating stops. In addition, as children are shamed by disempowering abuse and get a very negative sense of self, they have great difficulty believing that they are precious, lovable children of God.

When abuse is empowering, children worship the abusive parent. People abused by empowerment have a difficult time facing the fact that the empowering parent was abusive. They can hardly see that what happened between them was less than nurturing. This is true because the children—even as adults—need to protect the parent who made them feel so wonderful, so "better than." This worship often disguises both the child abuse and the parent's imperfections. These children may never see the fact that their parent was acting as the Higher Power.

Through empowering abuse children are given a false sense of being better than others. By the time they reach adulthood, they have become their own Higher Power. Though seldom this stark or conscious, the empowered child's attitude is, "I am a (better-than-others) Higher Power. I can do whatever I want to do. I am entitled to take from others, use others, and act shamelessly to get my will done." When children become their own Higher Power and believe they are entitled to offend and shame others, they are seriously cut off from experiences of spirituality.

Sometimes children are angry with and hate the family concept of the Higher Power for allowing the parent to abuse them. The real issue is not that the Higher Power has allowed anything to happen, but that the offender has been abusive. But the children can blame the Higher Power to protect themselves from facing the unacceptable and painful reality that the offending adult (in whom their security lay) is the one who hurt them. This scenario can create strong denial in the child about the parent's abusive behavior and sometimes profound delusion. And of course this blaming of God can create an enormous resistance to the idea of surrendering to a Higher Power later.

SOME NOT SO OBVIOUS EXAMPLES

Overcontrolling. When children are born, they don't know who they are or how to do anything. They begin to get a sense of who they are and how to do things by noticing what the parents are doing and who the parents are.

Somewhere between the ages of eighteen months and three years, children start wanting to do things their own way. If the parents do not allow the children to start this separation process and continue it until the time they are adults, the children are being overcontrolled.

If the parent demands that the children do or believe only exactly what the parent does and that anything else is unacceptable, the children may never go through that developmental process in which they learn to feel good about doing things their way. If this squelching of the children's freedom to become unique individual selves is carried to the extreme, the children lose touch with any sense of what their own way is. Such children and later adults have to wait for other people to tell them how to do almost anything new. They also have a difficult time being spontaneous or creative and are bound to limited and predictable responses.

When these children become adults they have a hard time figuring out how to do anything without a rigid set of rules. Some of them look for a marriage or a church in which there will be strict rules to be adhered to.

Providing an inhuman set of rules. A functional family provides a set of rules for the children that are humanly possible to follow and that the parents follow. These rules eventually become the foundation for the child's value system. The two most important requirements for healthy functional rules is that they are clear and that they can be followed by human beings. Inhuman rules are rules that nobody can live up to. With regard to child abuse, exactly what the specific rules are is not so crucial as long as the child has some way of knowing what they are and that they are perceived as doable because other family members adhere to the same rules. This is not to say that "any rule will do," but I am here addressing the issue of the necessity for clear, doable, functional rules.

A dysfunctional family provides the children with no rules or such vague or contradictory rules that life is chaotic. Or if there are any reasonable rules the parents expect the children to follow, they don't follow the rules themselves. They say in effect, "Do as we say and not as we do. We don't have to follow the rules. We are above them. We're god and goddess of the family." For example, a parent smokes cigarettes but says to the kids, "Don't you ever smoke."

With inhuman rules and values children are continually trying to achieve something that cannot be achieved and therefore constantly failing and getting shamed. They come to believe that God also expects them to live up to rules they can never follow and they have a sense that they are not "good enough" for God to love them, honor them, or help them.

Demanding perfection. As we saw in Chapter 4, children are imperfect people. To teach them that being perfect is normal is dysfunctional. Perhaps this teaching is not stated so plainly, but the parents' obvious expectation that their children never make a mistake, come home with a low grade, or lose anything can have the same abusive effect. When children live in families that expect perfection, they learn to lie (to avoid the pain and shame of frequent failure) or to repress the fact that they are imperfect. And this means these children can't be accountable and spiritual as adults, since they cannot tolerate *seeing* the mistakes and sabotaging behavior in their own lives.

Expecting children to be adultlike when they're children is dysfunctional because their very nature is childlike. Expecting a child to be an adult is about as useless as expecting a caterpillar to fly like a butterfly. Some special children will work very hard at being perfect and adultlike, but they often get traumatized because they inevitably fail to do everything "right." They become perfectionists or even work addicts as adults and are miserable, frequently failing, seldom able to enjoy their successes, and eternally hating themselves because they're not perfect.

Consequently they grow up with a distorted but strong sense that they are failing all the time because they are not meeting the impossible and illusive mark that moves always ahead of them across life like a mirage across the desert. And the grownup children shame themselves as adults for behavior that is often simply "being human."

Perfectionism is dysfunctional. Since I have been deafened by the message that I have to "do everything perfectly" I developed a wonderful motto several years ago that helps me stop insisting on doing things perfectly: "If it's worth doing, it's worth doing poorly—but it is worth getting done."

Abandonment. Abandonment creates spiritual abuse. Abandoned children are left to parent themselves. Lacking guidance from an adult, abandoned children's idealistic thinking may lead them to believe they are perfect, and can be their own Higher Power, blocking their spirituality. People who see themselves as being perfect put themselves in the "better-than" position from which experiencing a Higher Power is almost impossible.

Another reason abandonment is spiritually abusive is that most abandoned children cannot grasp the concept of a Higher Power who will be actively involved in their lives, since no caregiver interacted with them. They either believe that there is no Higher Power or they don't trust the Higher Power to support and help them.

No information about true spirituality. A dysfunctional family system neglects to give information to the children about what true spirituality is. Children learn about spirituality from their parents. Functional parents might begin by explaining how spirituality or faith works for them.

Parents who refuse to admit mistakes. Most dysfunctional parents refuse to apologize or make amends when they make a mistake—even a really obvious one. Parents who refuse to embrace their own shame and be accountable teach the children that they can offend others without experiencing their own natural shame. Since natural shame is the emotion that leads people to accountability, people repressing their natural shame have great difficulty experiencing spirituality, which requires the ability to be accountable.

WHEN A CHILD'S PARENTS ARE ADDICTED TO RELIGION

An addiction is a compulsive process designed to distract one from intolerable reality. Because it has the power to mask the pain of life, whatever the addiction is becomes the highest priority in a person's life, taking time and attention away from other priorities such as children.

Religious addicts use religion or God like a drug to empower themselves, control their environment, and relieve unbearable reality (feelings, thoughts, physical attributes, or pains). Because religion or God does relieve the pain, like any addictive process, these people overuse it. Because the addiction to religion gains power over them and takes time and attention away from other priorities, including any children they may have, religious addicts almost always abuse their children, because their focus is on the addiction and not on the children who need time, attention, direction, and love from the parents.

Religious addicts primarily abuse their children through neglect. They may become "religious workaholics," be away from the family doing things at church, studying books or the Bible, speaking or teaching, volunteering to care for the needy when their own children's need for them goes unnoticed.

Second, religious addicts often use the concept of God as a way to frighten and threaten the children. The children's fear of God's punishment forces them to do what the parents want them to do. The parents overcontrol the children, and the children learn to be afraid of God. This can be complicated when the parents *talk about* God's "being in charge" when in fact the child *experiences* the parents as always trying to get their own way.

Third, many religious addicts avoid any real problem solving with their children by quoting Bible verses. I am not making disparaging remarks about quoting Bible verses. I read the Bible and find much comfort and wonderful rich spiritual gifts in it. But when parents are addicts, they are most often empty, frightened, and childlike. Such parents have nothing to teach the children about life from their own substance. Instead of providing structure for their children in the form of rules and information that they can understand, these parents just quote Bible verses that children can't understand. Children's immature minds are not equipped to understand deep, religious, ethical concepts. But these things are quoted to children often without any explanation of what the quotation might mean to them at their stage of development. Bible quoting like this can give children an underlying message of, "If you were competent you'd understand what I'm saying and what God wants you to do." In that experience the children get confused, angry, and shamed because they can't understand what the parent is trying to tell them.

Many religious addicts demonstrate irresponsibility to children by turning everything over to God without doing any footwork. The attitude I'm describing is, "I'm helpless and have no responsibility to take action in my life. It's all up to God." I believe in turning over my concerns to a Higher Power. But along with that act and often preceding it there is a lot of footwork *I* have to do. Children need to see what human responsibility looks like—even for those who depend on a Higher Power—so they can learn how to solve problems and live their lives effectively. When parents just turn everything over without doing anything about the problem themselves, children learn nothing about how to approach life's problems. When they grow up they are ill-equipped to face life on life's terms.

Another dysfunctional maxim many religious addicts hold is that their children and any other people who are having problems are having them because they are not "right" with God. Immature children who cannot know that this maxim is not correct blame themselves for every problem they have, often including the abusive behavior of their parents. They believe their problems and the abuse they suffer are their own fault for not being right with God. As a result, God becomes a symbol of punishment for children in such families. In addition to seeing God as "punisher," children taught this way often learn to be very judgmental and lose their ability to be spiritual.

People who are right with God still have problems—and a spiritual relationship with a Higher Power to guide them through the problems. Real life is full of problems.

I used to think that in recovery I wouldn't have problems—I'd never get jealous, never have rage attacks, never have fights with my ex-husband. I'd figure out in advance everything that could be dysfunctional, make a plan and follow it, and life would go smoothly. I've found the opposite to be true—I seem to have more problems. Of course, I don't actually have more problems, but I have more *awareness of reality* and therefore of life's problems. I also am getting in touch with more joy and less fear, and many good feelings about myself.

Religiously addicted parents often teach the children that God is a punishing, strict, demanding God who expects rigid adherence to a set of rules. In so doing, they also teach the children that there is only *one way* to think about certain issues, because that's "what God has told us to think." If the children don't think about an issue the way the parents do, then the children are not spiritually acceptable and God will punish them.

Children who have one or both parents who are religious addicts have great difficulty challenging anything the parent does or says that they disagree with. They have the sense that confronting this religious addict parent is actually disagreeing with and complaining about God himself. Spiritually abused people have extreme difficulty confronting and being angry with religious addict parents and knowing that these parents are sick because the parents' addiction is about things pertaining to God.

I can tell from the descriptions spiritually abused patients give of their parent that the parent is a religious addict. The patients' resistance to facing this issue is usually so strong and stormy because it's extremely frightening for them to admit how painful and abusive it really was in the home everyone said was so spiritual.

In any Twelve-Step program, spirituality is a key to successful recovery. If people don't have a sense of a supporting, caring power greater than themselves and greater than their parents, they often have a very hard time even getting started into recovery. And since I believe that a Twelve-Step program is imperative for recovery from codependence, facing issues of spiritual abuse can be crucial to a successful treatment program.

PHYSICAL, SEXUAL, OR EMOTIONAL ABUSE FROM A RELIGIOUS REPRESENTATIVE

It is highly distressful for a child to receive physical, sexual, or emotional abuse from a religious representative. Among the patients who come to The Meadows for chemical addiction, food addiction, and/or codependence treatment, a significant number write about being sexually abused by spiritual or religious leaders, male and female. Abuse is also perpetrated by doctors, counselors, therapists, and other people in the helping professions.

Religious leaders are not immune to having a sex addiction. And I think sex addiction can be more easily hidden in a religious context, because many very vulnerable people come to religious professionals privately for spiritual care and guidance. The religious leader can act out his or her sex addiction in relative safety and secrecy with these very needy people, because nobody would think that kind of thing would happen with a religious professional. Victims have great resistance to revealing a sexual offender. And sometimes, even if the abused person does try to tell someone, he or she is not believed.

In contrast to spiritual abuse by a parent, the religious professional does not usually become the child's Higher Power. But more often, because the spiritual leader is a representative of God, the child hates or is angry with God for allowing the abuse to happen. Or the child is afraid, and has an attitude that "being connected to the Higher Power means I am going to be hurt because of what took place, and I am afraid of the Higher Power because he allowed that to happen to me."

Sexual abuse from a religious representative is especially destructive. Having dealt with many people sexually abused by a religious representative, I believe that whenever this happens, an act of profound evil is occurring. I find that many of the victims at some point hover between life and death in recovery wrestling with the question, "Am I going to make a decision to live or kill myself?" Most of the time they are not consciously grappling with suicide, but when they confront their history, it's obvious that they are dealing with an issue of life and death magnitude.

In treatment as soon as the memories of sexual abuse surface these patients often feel intense trauma and pain. It is hard to own the reality that a representative of God did something so shaming and abusive to you. Just the experience of "really knowing it fully" makes the patients very uncomfortable. But they must proceed and embrace the knowledge that they really were violated by someone who was supposed to be safe and represented such an immense power as God. Most people get devastated and become very angry. But there are so many admonitions against and fears about being angry with God, that it's hard to allow oneself to feel this anger. Most patients turn this anger in on themselves, becoming extremely depressed and suicidal. It's really hard to help them give themselves permission to feel their feelings and to say whatever they have to say to their Higher Power or God to get themselves free of the enormous residual feelings. The inner decision to face and deal with the feelings surrounding this kind of spiritual sexual abuse represents a real spiritual crisis. But neither recovery nor true spirituality can be found until the resistance is overcome.

I know that if I didn't have spirituality in my recovery I probably would have killed myself by now. More than anything else, recovery is about the development of authentic spirituality, a wonderful thing. But if a person has been abused by a spiritual leader, the ability to turn to the spiritual gifts in the program is greatly retarded. There is no trust in a Higher Power and it's very hard to let go and get oneself through the steps. I have a friend who considers suicide all the time. She cannot reconcile the awful things that happened to her as a result of some very serious sexual abuse by a priest. She cannot seem to make use of the spiritual gifts in the program because of all the anger and pain that stand between her and the Higher Power. In my opinion, based on my experiences with many survivors, physical, emotional, and spiritual abuse at the hands of a spiritual leader lead to the very, very serious consequenes of denial, delusion, and repression. But sexual abuse by them is even more severe and harder to treat.

CODEPENDENCE: WHAT IT IS, WHERE IT COMES FROM, HOW IT SABOTAGES OUR LIVES

As we have seen, less-than-nurturing or dysfunctional parenting techniques create abused children who adapt into codependent adults. The abuse may have been blatant and obvious or more subtle and hidden, but its effects on us are real and disruptive to our lives and relationships. And as we have seen, society's acceptance of childcare practices has turned out to be a poor standard by which to judge whether a particular technique is beneficial to a child.

Our own recovery from the abusive experiences we had in our families of origin will improve the quality of our own lives and also those of our children. The healing effect on any boys and girls we may work with anywhere can be greatly enhanced—in school, Scouts, church, or day care. We can learn to pay more attention to the impact we have on these valuable, vulnerable, imperfect, dependent, and immature little people. But all positive change for codependents begins as we come out of denial and delusion about our own condition and history and treat ourselves first. As we recover we will automatically begin to be able to give more nurturing and appropriate care to children and be more intimate with others around us.

We've now seen an overall picture of codependence, where it came from in our childhood experiences and how it operates in our lives as adults. Although it is clear that we did not "cause" our codependence, many of us have an attitude of self-contempt and disgust because we seem to be so "immature and stupid." Part of recovery for me has been to recognize that we are in a state of disease and we had no control over the childhood circumstances that led to our present adult discomfort.

Learning about the diseases and then *taking responsibility for our own recovery* are the doorways to a new life. Facing codependence is the first big step, but how can we begin to heal these childhood wounds and mature into functional adults?

Part 4

MOVING TOWARD RECOVERY

CHAPTER 15

Personal Recovery

It's important to me to do more than describe codependence and how it apparently develops from childhood abuse. But because of the complex nature of the disease and its connection to child abuse, I have concentrated in this book on presenting a full discussion of the roots and the symptoms of the disease. In this last part I want to outline the process of recovery from codependence, a process that I treated at length in a workbook (with Andrea Wells Miller) called *Breaking Free: A Recovery Workbook for Facing Codependence*.

I'm aware that it can feel overwhelming when someone describes the illness and you recognize that you have it. But there is a great deal of hope and promise that we codependents can have functional and fulfilling relationships. More and more has been learned about the disease and how to treat it. At this time there are more experienced therapists working with codependents than there have ever been. There are many people in recovery who can demonstrate the strength of the recovery process and ways to grow in it. I strongly recommend that you consult a therapist and attend a Twelve-Step group such as Codependents Anonymous to begin to familiarize yourself with the ways codependence works in your life and with sound paths to recovery.

FACING CODEPENDENCE

The first step in facing codependence is to see and acknowledge its symptoms in our own lives. As we begin to face these symptoms and try to change lifelong behaviors, we will run into powerful resistance and irrational feelings. That's just part of recovery from this disease. But the first step is to check the symptoms against our own behavior.

As we've seen, the primary symptoms of codependence are experienced at opposite extremes. As a review, they are:

Experiencing low or nonexistant self esteem	or	An arrogant & grandiose stance
Being too vulnerable	or	Being invulnerable
Being bad/rebellious	or	Being good/perfect
Being too dependent	or	Being antidependent, or needless/wantless
Being chaotic	or	Being controlling

CHARACTERISTICS OF RECOVERING CODEPENDENTS

Whichever column of characteristics we exhibit, as we move into recovery we have the sense that we are taking a flight into the traits of the opposite column. As we move from little or no self-esteem to esteeming ourselves in a healthy way, the thought comes that perhaps we are being arrogant. As we move from being too vulnerable to setting appropriate boundaries, we think perhaps we are becoming invulnerable and distant. As we move away from a rebellious approach to life we fear becoming too perfect. As we stop being clinging and dependent we believe perhaps we may become antidependent. And as we move away from chaos toward structure and responsibility we may feel as if we are becoming too controlling.

For people coming into recovery from the other extreme, moving away from arrogance feels like a journey into low or no self-esteem. Moving away from being invulnerable and risking vulnerability feels like "too much" vulnerability, because it is unfamiliar (and uncomfortable). Getting less "good and perfect" feels like becoming rebellious and "bad," and as we let up on our control the resulting experiences may seem to be chaotic.

It's helpful to note that although recovery feels like we are moving too far in an opposite direction, we probably are not. A perfectionist woman who leaves her dirty dishes in the sink overnight may feel chaotic but in reality she is not. Recovery *feels* extreme because functional behavior feels so unfamiliar to us after years of living in the experience of codependence, no matter which extreme we may be coming from. And these experiences of "not knowing what's normal" are *all* necessary parts of recovery, as we learn by listening and sharing in meetings and with our sponsor.

Certain characteristics of a healthy person begin to appear as a codependent confronts each core symptom and gets in recovery. Some of these are:

Self-esteeming from within

Vulnerable, but with protection

Accountable for imperfections and spiritual; able to look to a Higher Power for help with imperfections

Interdependent

Experiencing reality in moderation.

RECOVERY BEGINS WITH PAIN

Without some sort of painful consequences resulting from our dysfunctional behaviors, it doesn't usually occur to us that we need to change. Codependents don't just wake up one day saying, "I think I'll move over into maturity and mental health." For example, it may not hurt to be in the arrogant, isolated position, and such people may see no reason to change. If their families are going crazy trying to live with them, or they have no close intimate relationships, arrogant ones usually assume the problems in the family or in any relationship are about the other people and consider themselves to be "fine."

The confrontation brought about by a successful intervention or treatment causes people to move out of the arrogant set of symptoms into pain. Exposing the arrogant, invulnerable, perfectionist, antidependent, and controlling behaviors as being dysfunctional adaptations lead to intense pain and fear. But people have to be in this sort of pain to be willing to do the work necessary to begin recovery. This painful phase of recovery is *not* a permanent way of life. Codependents need courage and a relationship to a Higher Power to continue this stage of recovery and keep growing until they move through it into a more comfortable position.

That brings up another point especially for people who haven't gotten into recovery yet and are hovering on the verge of considering it: if you get into recovery, the first year or so will probably be very painful. You will have the paradoxical experience of being glad to be in recovery but also feeling worse.

I have discovered that we codependents are very hard to treat. I resisted doing anything people suggested that might have gotten me into recovery sooner. It wasn't until I experienced enough pain to become willing to do *anything* to change that I would try their suggestions.

I mention this because I had no one to tell me that the early stages of recovery include a lot of pain as one quits running from fears and feelings and faces codependence. I was baffled by feeling both joy and increased pain. I did a lot of my own recovery by myself. The only people who knew I was working on my recovery were the patients I was talking to, because at first I wasn't trying to be a professional with them. I was being who I was, a suffering fellow codependent trying to get well. I noticed that as I started doing the things I had to do to get better, I felt worse and worse—even though I had incredible feelings of joy and hope about *finally* seeing what had been happening to me all these years.

UNEXPECTED FEARS AND UNCERTAINTIES

Besides the pain and joy, there were some fears and uncertainties I hadn't counted on. For instance, when I started into recovery I was quite a perfectionist. I was overmature and controlling. I felt old and worn out. It was as if I were thirty-six going on eighty. When I let go of being controlling I became like a very immature, chaotic child, whining like a baby all the time and engaging in amazing immature behavior I never thought I was capable of. It was behavior I'd never done before, because I never was a child.

Yet I was deluded about my behavior and couldn't see that it was childish and self-centered. The idea that I could choose not to be the way I always had been was a heady trip. But every now and then I'd break through that delusion because my husband or my surrogate mom would confront it. My surrogate mom would say something like, "You know, it's hard to be in a relationship with you because you're so self-centered. You never call me. I always have to call you." It was really painful, because I love this woman.

Perhaps the most painful and uncertain experience for me was when I moved from needlessness to experiencing my needs. I became aware for the first time of what my needs were and also that I knew how to take care of very few of them—almost none. I found it very painful even to admit I *had* the needs, much less to set out to get them met. And when I began to be more vulnerable, I felt as if I were unprotected and that everything that came at me would destroy me.

But fortunately it gets better—a lot better. After over six years of being in a recovery process, I live much of my life in the recovery set of characteristics listed earlier in this chapter. And the pain and shame about the past and the fear that I'll never be all right have been replaced by a serenity based on the hope I'm experiencing. I'm discovering this hope through my Higher Power, the tools of recovery included in the Twelve Steps, and my recovering friends. But of course I don't stay there all the time.

Recovery for me means living in the recovery characteristics more than in the codependence characteristics. Everyone I know working a recovery program has imperfect recovery. In fact, as I try to be in *perfect* recovery I get entangled in the disease of codependence again. I slip into my disease on a regular basis, but the difference is that I don't stay there as long as I used to. Now acting codependently hurts me quickly and acutely, so I get out of it as soon as I can.

CODEPENDENCE WILL NOT GO AWAY ON ITS OWN

As I mentioned in the beginning, in the groups I lead and with the codependents I know well, I often say, "Hug your demons or they'll bite you in the ass." To get well we must begin addressing codependence in our lives and do something about our own codependent demons. If we expect anybody else—even a good therapist—to do our recovery *for* us we will stay stuck, lost, and sick. No one else can do this work for us, and no one is meant to. Although our parents were the ones who should have helped us by exposing us to functional reality and respectful caregiving, there is no need to blame them today. Once the damage has been done, our parents cannot make it right or fix us. We each have to learn how to recover on our own.

It is my hope that as we begin to recogize the core symptoms operating in ourselves (which I believe is the place to begin), and see how the harmful consequences happen in our lives, we can begin to do two things. First we can begin to learn how to intervene on the disease in our own lives: to treat ourselves with more respect, to develop boundaries, to own our reality, to become responsible for our own wants and needs, and to begin to approach life with moderation. Second, we can learn how to become better caregivers to our own children: how to appropriately esteem them, how to avoid abusing them and teach them to have intact boundaries, how to allow them to have their own reality and guide them to more maturity, how to appropriately nurture them, and how to provide a stable environment for them as they develop into adulthood.

If your children have already become adults then the second task will be to learn how to operate at your end of the relationship in recovery. I've often heard it said, and I believe it strongly: the best thing we can do for our adult children is to get into recovery for ourselves and set them free to find their own way to recovery. We can live in recovery and model it, but once our children are adults, they must be free to live their own lives. We may be accountable for their codependence, but we cannot be responsible for its cure, in that we cannot make them do what it takes to recover. A sign of our own recovery will be the willingness to learn the difference between modeling a recovered life and sharing our own strength and hope, and crossing our adult children's boundaries to insist that they live life our way, even if it is a life of recovery. Just as our parents cannot be in charge of our own recovery, so we cannot "make" our children well or "give" them any of our own recovery.

TWELVE-STEP MEETINGS

First, consider attending a Twelve-Step meeting where you can be with some people who are talking about the disease and recovery from it. Codependents Anonymous (CoDA) is a Twelve-Step program based on the same Twelve Steps used by Alcoholics Anonymous. At the time I am writing this, new groups are being organized in many parts of the country. If you are interested in starting such a group, you can get a starter's kit by writing to Codependents Anonymous, P.O. Box 33577, Phoenix, Arizona 85067-3557.

I want to emphasize the importance of talking not only about the illness of codependence and how it operates in one's life, but also about what your recovery is like when you experience it. It's not productive to talk only about the disease and how it's making your life unmanageable. Talking about the positive experiences you are having as you start experiencing glimpses of recovery will help you focus your awareness on your own progress and improvement as well as give valuable experience, strength, and hope to others. Learning how to work the Twelve Steps to recovery is also very important.

A WRITTEN STEP ONE

A second thing that helps many codependents into recovery through the Twelve-Step process is to do a "written Step One." Step One as adapted for codependents reads as follows: "We admitted we were powerless over others and that our lives had become unmanageable."

The purpose of Step One is to help us *see the disease in action in ourselves*. Until we see the disease working in our own lives and relationships, it's almost impossible to do anything about it. There are two parts to this step. (1) Writing about how we experience each core symptom explained in chapter 2 shows the specific way we experience powerlessness over codependence in our lives. (2) Writing about what happens as a result—the five types of sabotage explained in chapter 3—describes how our lives are unmanageable. It can take quite a while to do this, but this writing goes a long way to help us see our particular patterns of codependence. There are more details about how I suggest doing this and the rest of the steps in *Breaking Free: A Recovery Workbook for Facing Codependence*.

A CODEPENDENCE SPONSOR

A third thing you can do for yourself is get a codependence sponsor. I would suggest that you choose someone who has spent some time in recovery and demonstrates functional behavior with respect to some of his or her codependence symptoms. But given these qualifications, the most important characteristic of a good codependence sponsor is someone who can parent and nurture you, who is honest and confrontive, willing to tell you how you look but also able to repeat things over and over until you get them. The disease makes us "forget" much of what is told us about ourselves. So you need a patient, nurturing, parenting person. I would suggest that you get a member of the same sex unless you are homosexual.

As a matter of fact I strongly urge you *not* to try to do your codependence sponsor work with a member of the opposite sex. You may wind up "Thirteenth Stepping" each other (geting into a romantic or sexual relationship), which is inappropriate and dysfunctional for your own recovery and the sponsor's.

CONFRONT EACH SYMPTOM

Fourth, confront within yourself each symptom I described at the beginning of this book: low or nonexistent self-esteem, impaired boundaries, owning your reality, meeting your own needs and wants, and operating in extremes. However, it's very difficult to know and continue to keep in mind what the problems are unless you do a written Step One.

Codependence is an insidious and subtle disease. If you find that you are unable to take the steps I have suggested, you may want to talk to a counselor who works with codependents. (Many therapists are *not* familiar with the disease as such or the recovery techniques that have been discovered the last few years.) You may be able to locate a good therapist or counselor by calling a chemical dependency treatment center. Many such centers now have resident or outpatient treatment programs for codependence that can be very helpful for people who are serious about wanting to be in recovery from the disease.

We have used the term "disease" throughout this book to describe codependence, yet it is not a disease like the flu or pneumonia for which we seek a cure and get well. Recovery from codependence is more like being in remission from something like diabetes. As long as a diabetic continues to follow the prescribed treatment of diet, exercise, and perhaps doses of insulin, he or she can lead as active a life as a nondiabetic. But if the diabetic does not follow his or her regimen, a diabetic relapse can occur at any time. In a similar way, as long as we follow a recovery program, we can lead more healthy, functional lives. But we are subject to relapse when we start thinking we are "well" and no longer need to work a recovery program.

But whatever tack you take, I urge you to make a beginning now in facing codependence. Hundreds of people are already in recovery as I am writing these words to you. We were afraid, lonely, resentful, and discouraged women and men who could not get our lives and relationships straightened out. Many of us had almost lost hope that we would ever be happy. And now, although it seems miraculous to us—we are getting well. Come and join us!

To contact Pia Mellody about speaking engagements, write or call Mellody Enterprises, P.O. Box 1739, Wickenburg, AZ 85358 (602) 684-5075.

To contact J. Keith Miller about speaking engagements, write or call Michael McKinney, McKinney Associates, Inc., P.O. Box 5162, Louisville, KY 40205, (502) 583-8222.

Appendix

A Brief History of Codependence and a Look at the Psychological Literature

As we mentioned in the Foreword, understanding of the symptoms of what we are now calling codependence first surfaced in a notable way in the chemical dependency field in the treatment of the families of alcoholics. While no one seems to know with any certainty where the term "codependence" or "codependency" came from, it is generally thought to have evolved from "co-alcoholic" when alcoholism and other drug dependencies began being spoken of together as "chemical dependence."

At first the symptoms of codependence were thought to be caused by the stress of living with an addicted person. The exaggerated shame, fear, pain, and anger of the family members were seen as reactions to a very sick man or woman who was out of control because of his or her chemical addiction.

But as alcoholics got sober the codependent behaviors of their families often *continued* and sometimes even escalated. It became apparent there was a separate disease operating in the family members. The hidden causes of this disease, therapists soon realized, might very well have predated the alcoholic's drinking.

As more family members went for therapy and revealed the histories of their families of origin, it became clear that many of the codependent spouses had one or two alcoholic parents. And the adult child subsequently seemed to unconsciously *choose* an alcoholic or addict as a spouse (some even made this choice serially in several marriages). It appeared there was something familiar in the *abusive pattern of behavior* of the alcoholic (or mate who was to become an alcoholic) that allowed the codependent spouse to reconstitute an earlier abusive situation in his or her childhood that had perhaps been repressed. Although it happened unconsciously, it was as if by reconstituting the earlier abuse situation the codependent spouse could now get (besides the security of the familiar) another chance to be "perfect" or "pleasing" enough to free himself or herself from the exaggerated shame, fear, pain, and anger that had been carried since childhood. It came out that these feelings had colored and crippled many of the codependents' relationships for a lifetime.

As people began to deal with their symptoms of codependence at treatment centers, conferences, and in therapy sessions, the evidence became irrefutable that the codependent did *not* have to have a chemically dependent person in his or her life at all, either as a child or as an adult to have the disease of codependence. It was enough to have had an abusive caregiver as a child. In this book we have tried to describe a connection between that childhood abuse and the adult symptoms of codependence.

CODEPENDENCE AS A DISEASE

Unlike most "discoveries" of new diseases, codependence surfaced in the arena of chemical dependency and is filtering very slowly *back* into the rest of the mental health field, from where such discoveries usually come. Professionals in the chemical dependency field have focused on grass-roots, practical approaches to therapy not closely identified with academically or theoretically oriented Ph.D. research programs. Because of this practical focus there has been little effort to fit the significant breakthroughs and methodology or conceptualizations regarding codependence into the language or structure of academic psychology.

A BRIEF LOOK AT THE PSYCHOLOGICAL LITERATURE: PSYCHOLOGICAL ABSTRACTS

To prepare for writing this book the authors searched the data base of the psychological abstracts on a compact disk. These abstracts include articles from all sorts of psychological journals representing the cutting edge of psychological research and new developments. Since codependence is a new phenomenon, having surfaced by name only in the past few years, we checked all the abstracts and pertinent articles from January 1983 to September 1988 (inclusive). This led to the discovery that traditional psychological literature contains only a few references to the disease of codependence, at least by name.

The following eight articles pertaining to "codependence" or "codependency" were all published since 1985.

Lans Lesater et al. (1985), examined family and social problems of clients at a community clinic, including chemical use patterns. The survey comparing random patients and those receiving mental health care indicates that thirty-nine percent of those receiving mental health care had one member of the family using drugs at the "circumstantial-situational" level as compared to thirty percent of the total clinical group. The author concludes that chemical use and associated problems such as codependence are significant factors affecting families.

Sydney Walter (1986) presents a case in which the wife of a male alcoholic learned to detach herself from her husband's drinking.

Jean Caldwell (1986) presents guidelines for working with codependent families and getting them ready for intervention. The author emphasizes that challenging dysfunctional behavior in an alcoholic is only successful when combined with supporting his healthy behavior.

Neil M. Rothberg (1986) presents a family systems approach to alcoholism by examining the dynamics working within marital subsystems, three family-oriented models, and possible treatment and goals. Both spouses are shown to be contributors to the alcoholic problem and both are affected by it.

Gierymski and Williams (1986) state that wives (and probably other members) in families with an alcoholic member are more likely to suffer emotional problems than the families of nonalcoholics, although the exact degree and form of their emotional problems vary and no clear-cut entity corresponding precisely to the concept of codependence has emerged. In short the authors express skepticism concerning the validity of the concept of codependence.

Timmon Cermak in the *Journal of Psychoactive Drugs* (1986) argues that codependence can be defined within the DSM-III criteria for mixed personality disorder. He proposes five diagnostic criteria in the style of DSM-III. According to Cermak

the essential features of codependency include (1) continual investment of self-esteem in the ability to influence/control feelings and behavior in self and others in the face of obvious adverse consequences; (2) assumption of responsibility for meeting other's needs to the exclusion of acknowledging one's own needs; (3) anxiety and boundary distortions in situations of intimacy and separation; (4) enmeshment in relationships with personality disordered, drug dependent and impulse disordered individuals; and (5) exhibits (in any combinations of three or more) constriction or emotions with or without dramatic outbursts, depression, hypervigilance, compulsions, anxiety, excessive reliance on denial, substance abuse, recurrent physical or sexual abuse, stress-related medical illness, and/or a primary relationship with an active substance abuser for at least two years without seeking outside support.

Cermak takes each criterion and points out how it relates to established DSM diseases (e.g., Dependent Personality Disorder, Borderline Personality Disorder, Histrionic Personality Disorder).

Cermak alone in the psychological literature searched has tried to describe codependence and present a case for its deserving serious consideration as a disease.

Sondra Smalley (1987) discussed dependency issues in lesbian relationships. Although not particularly helpful in describing what codependence is, the author proposes a model that focuses on the client's intervention in her own codependent relationship patterns.

Frederich A. Prezioso (1987) discusses spirituality as it relates to the treatment of chemically dependent and codependent people in a 21–28 day inpatient treatment setting. The author suggests addressing spiritual issues using staff training sessions and weekly staff groups, patient lectures and discussion groups, family presentations, and individualized treatment plans.

In trying to determine what research had been done (under other headings) on the cluster of symptoms we are calling codependence, we checked the *Thesaurus of Psychological Index Terms* (1985). This thesaurus (which contains all the subject headings under which articles are listed in the psychological abstracts) does not contain any references to either "codependence" or "codependency." A check of all the articles recorded in the abstracts under the heading "dependency (personality)" and "child abuse" (the headings relating most nearly to what we are describing here) for the January 1983 to September 1988 period revealed that very little has been considered worthy of inclusion in those abstracts that pertains to the identifiable diagnosis of the disorder and symptoms we are calling codependence and its connection with child abuse.

In all the psychological literature appearing in the Psych-Lit data base during the period from January 1983 to September 1988 there seems to be only one person's work (used as a reference by several writers) that sees in the category "dependency (personality)" something close to what we are talking about when we speak of codependence. As a matter of fact all the references we found that related "dependency" to the symptoms that make up what we are calling codependence cited the same book, *Neurosis in Human*

Growth, by psychiatrist Karen Horney (1950). Some of her insights and descriptions of symptoms are similar to those in this volume but evidently they were never developed or expanded in subsequent literature in the direction we are pointing.

Horney saw healthy adults as autonomous to a great extent but believed that ultimately all people find survival difficult without the physical and emotional presence, support, and caring of others. Such *interdependence* enables us to grow and thrive and is necessary to the realization of individuality.

Neurosis, however, leads to seeking both fulfillment and a sense of one's self from other people. Relating to others becomes increasingly compulsive and may take the form of blind dependency, rebellion, the need to excel, or avoidance of involvement at all costs. In all these ways, neurotics demonstrate the importance others have for them.

Such dependence is usually characterized by inflexibility in relating, abdication of responsibility for one's own life, intolerance, depression, rage, and vindictiveness when one's demands on others are not met, indiscriminate sacrifice of one's own best interests, and a magical belief that one will find an answer to life through others. Dependence can be seen as a way of experiencing and relating to others that is a part of the particular character structure Horney calls "the self-effacing solution" (in chapter 9 of the book cited).

Security, meaningfulness of life, and a sense of self are believed by the neurotic to be attainable only through the strength and caring of others. Therefore moving toward others may reach the point of wishing to lose oneself and merge totally with another person. Consequently, being lovable, helpless, self-effacing, and small is cultivated and glorified in such people. Strength and autonomy, while sought in a protector, are shunned and repressed in oneself. Evaluation of oneself depends on lovableness; love, especially erotic love, offers the promise of supreme fulfillment. The subdued helpless part of oneself is experienced as its very essence, and one's lovableness, loving sacrifice, and especially suffering are taken as justification for demanding total devotion in return.

What in most normal people is a desire to be loved becomes in this sort of neurotic a desperate drive and claim on others. Thus Horney chose to call the end stage of self-effacement, which includes these symptoms, *morbid dependency.*

But until very recently these ideas of Horney's about dependency (and later references to them) constitute almost the only link in the psychological journals to what we know as "codependence," and these ideas apparently were not developed in the direction we have taken.

BOOKS ON OTHER EARLIER REFERENCES TO DEPENDENT PERSONALITY PATTERNS

Theodore Millon says in the *Encyclopedia of Psychology,* vol. I (1984),

Despite the prevalence and well-known features of this personality pattern (dependent personality), only passing reference was made to it in official nosologies published prior to the 1980 *Diagnostic and Statistical Manual of Mental Disorders*, Third Edition (DSM III). Giving the disorder the status of a separate and major disorder, DSM III includes as its central feature behavior passively allowing others to take full responsibility for one's significant life activities, a characteristic traceable to the person's lack of self-confidence and to doubts concerning the ability to function independently.

As Millon points out, early on Emil Kraepelin (1913) in the eighth edition of his *Psychiatrie* had stressed the "irresoluteness of will" of these dependent patients and the ease with which they could be "seduced" by others.

Karl Abraham (1924) noted their typical belief that "there will always be some kind person . . . to care for them and give them everything they need."

Next came Horney's description (already cited), which is closest to what we are describing as codependence, though it addresses the issues from a different perspective and makes no connection with child abuse.

Later Erich Fromm presented a characterization similar to Horney's in *Man for Himself* (1947). Speaking of those exhibiting what he terms the "receptive orientation," Fromm pointed out that "they are dependent not only on authorities, but . . . for any kind of support. They feel lost when they are alone because they feel they cannot do anything without help."

Using a biosocial learning theory to deduce personality types, Theodore Millon lists in *Disorders of Personality* (1981) the following diagnostic criteria for dependent personalities: (1) characteristically docile and noncompetitive, and avoids social tension and conflicts (which Millon calls "pacific temperament"); (2) needs a stronger nurturing figure, and without one feels anxiously helpless; is often conciliatory, placating, and self-sacrificing ("interpersonal submissiveness"); (3) perceives self as weak, fragile, and ineffectual; exhibits lack of confidence by belittling own aptitudes and competencies ("inadequate self-image"); (4) reveals a naive or benign attitude toward interpersonal difficulties; smooths over troubling events ("Pollyanna cognitive style"); (5) prefers a subdued, uneventful, and passive lifestyle, and avoids self-assertion and refuses autonomous responsibilities ("initiative deficit").

It is clear that observations were made years ago of people debilitated by symptoms of codependence. But it is also evident that there was little follow-up on the earliest notation by Kraepelin in 1913.

It seems even the *term* "dependency" went out of favor. It was too "inclusive" and not amenable to the more precise calipers psychological researchers were trying to develop. As John C. Masters writes in *The International Encyclopedia of Psychiatry, Psychology and Neurology* (1977):

More recently there has been a growing tendency to eschew the use of dependency as a global concept because of its over-inclusiveness and poor utility in describing and analyzing the behavior of adults and children more than one or two years of age.

I think this is enough to indicate that mainline academic psychology has not done extensive work on "dependency" (as it relates to the "codependence" we are describing) as an identifiable personality disorder at least in its usual channels of communication. And it was not until this agonizing cluster of symptoms surfaced and multiplied in the chemical dependency field that any therapists could gather extensive data to see the scope and relatedness of the disorder. But codependence is now seen by many of us to constitute a painful, almost ubiquitous problem for certain groups in our society. We are, it seems, on a primitive frontier with regard to the investigation of a serious personality disorder.

BUT IS IT A "DISEASE"?

Is codependence a disease? As psychiatrist Timmen Cermak in *Diagnosing and Treating Codependence* (1986) points out, "Therapists in traditional mental health approaches have attempted to treat (separately) the symptoms of codependence, diagnosing clients as having anxiety disorders, depression, hysterical personality disorders, or dependent personality disorders, to name a few." Cermak also says,

Once we accept that codependence exists on a par with other personality disorders such as borderline, narcissistic and dependent personalities it should be clear that it deserves to be treated with the same level of sophistication.

But since neither the language nor the criteria used to describe codependence are consistent or organized into a generally accepted substantive framework by those who work with the disorder, it has been impossible to do the research required to establish scientific validity for viewing it as a legitimate personality "disease." Until this research is done, the psychological community's own rules forbid including codependence in the nomenclature as a disease.

In the meantime those of us who deal with people in the grips of the compulsive symptoms of codependence are not waiting for the official labeling of the disease. Whatever codependence is, it certainly *acts* like a disease. And as Cermak (p. 100) notes, "According to what we have learned it would seem at least to fit the usual descriptions of a disease (with discernible symptoms that are predictable, progressive, and debilitating)." As any contemporary bibliography on codependence (like Cermak's book, almost exclusively from the chemical dependency field) suggests, many therapists are struggling to give form and structure to the river of data about codependence and its symptoms that is overflowing the banks of chemical dependency treatment centers into the other mental health fields.

It is our hope that this book will help clarify some issues in this expanding search for healing as it relates to codependence.

REFERENCES

Abraham, K. (1924) The influence of oraleroticism on character formation. *Selected papers on Psychoanalysis*. London: Hogarth.

American Psychiatric Association. (1980) *Diagnostic and Statistical Manual of Mental Disorders* (3rd Ed.) Washington, DC.

Caldwell, J. (1986) Preparing a family for intervention. *Journal of Psychoactive Drugs*. *18*(1):57–59.

Cermak, T. L. (1986) Diagnostic criteria for codependency. *Journal of Psychoactive Drugs*. *18*(1):15–20.

_____. (1986) *Diagnosing and Treating Codependence*. Minneapolis, MN: Johnson Institute Books, p. 61.

Corsini, R. J. (Ed) (1984) *Encyclopedia of Psychology*, vol. 1. New York: John Wiley & Sons. p. 354.

Fromm, E. (1947) *Man for Himself*. New York: Rinehart.

Gierymski, T. & Williams, T. (1986) Codependency. *Journal of Psychoactive Drugs*. *18*(1):7–13.

Horney, K. (1950) *Neurosis in Human Growth*. New York: Norton.

Kraepelin, E. (1913) *Psychiatrie* (8th Ed). Leipzig: J. Barth.

Lesater, L., Hakanson, N. M., Scott, D. M. & Henderson, S. F. (1985) Identifying chemical use problems in a community clinic. *Journal of Drug Education*. 15(2):171–185.

Millon, T. (1981) *Disorders of Personality: DSM-III Axis II*. New York: Wiley-Interscience.

Prezioso, F. A. (1987) Spirituality in the recovery process. *Journal of Substance Abuse Treatment*. 4(3–4):233–238.

Rothberg, N. M. (1986) The alcoholic spouse and the dynamics of codependency. *Alcoholism-Treatment Quarterly*. 3(1):73–86.

Smalley, S. (1987) Dependency Issues in lesbian relationships. *Journal of Homosexuality*. 14(1–2):125–135.

Walter, S. (1986) Putting the codependent in charge: A compression approach to an alcoholic system. *Journal of Strategic and Systems Therapies*. 5(3):1–3.

Wolman, B. B. (ed) (1977) *The International Encyclopedia of Psychiatry, Psychology, Psychoanalysis and Neurology*. New York: Van Nostrand. 4:50.

Index